Dedication

Between the lines, I write my life observances.

I also dedicate the novel to my friend, Pat. She is now

departed from this world. She was my guiding light and

introduced me to the joy of writing.

I dedicate the book to employees that work for retail

corporations. You are my inspiration and incentive.

Under the Apron
Corporate Oligarchy and the 21st Century Economic Slave.

Contact Payton Lee at

http://www.paytonlee.com

Email: clancy811@gmail.com

This is a work of nonfiction. Names, characters, places, and incidents are factual with modifications to protect the guilty and innocent. The references, incidents, and personalities are factual and experienced by the author or given as experiences by workers in a oligarchic corporate society of the 21st Century. The instances refer to many large retail corporations over a period of nearly thirty years.

ISBN: 146816886X

PROLOGUE

Under the Apron became an inspiration after reading a book called the Hemingses of Monticello, the current economic unsolvable crisis, the catastrophic oil spill in the Gulf of Mexico with the corporation controlling the Federal and State Governments, and the media. There have been recent inspiring editorials, the banter of bloggers in internet news sites, news stories about foreign and domestic workers that have made headlines, personal experiences, employee experiences, and a TV series called "Undercover Boss." All of the above experiences in this time period have inspired me to scribe this personal record.

The disclaimer I wish to place in the front of this book is that these are strictly my perceptions. I cannot expect everyone to agree with my perceptions, nor do I ask anyone to do so. All of history is written documentation of an individual's perception. Accuracy, data, and evidence are prohibitive in the recording of history. Perceptions on the other hand, are abundant in historical documentation. This book is my desire to keep a record for historians in the next centuries of the life of American workers in the 21st century.

To me the most fascinating of my perceptions is that the Revolutionary War wasn't really about freedom or democracy. The Revolutionary War was simply about Rich White Men who didn't want to pay taxes. The Rich White Men just wanted to get richer and not share any of it with the current government. No, that isn't my brain child bit of wisdom. I heard that from a comedian and pondered it for some time. The comedian delivered the most accurate description of what had really occurred, not slanted patriotic flag waving historical writing. The comedian also added at the end of that sentence, "Nothing has changed." I perceive that to be a most accurate statement.

I studied the Revolutionary War in greater depth and I came to the conclusion that The United States of America, Constitution, and Bill of Rights was simply good marketing for the time. The United States was really a plutocracy and not a democracy as it claimed.

Plutocracy by definition is rule by a group of super wealthy elitists. The small percentage of wealthy would govern and rule the masses. It was not until well after the Revolutionary War that the common man was allowed to vote. The foundation of the United States was based on solely the vote of wealthy land and slave owners. Tennessee's entry into the United States as the sixteenth State changed the rule allowing other than wealthy landowners the right to vote and make laws. Andrew Jackson was one of those statesmen and later became President of the United States.

The wealthy landowners weren't too happy about this change but the tide was turned and the plutocracy began to develop into a democracy.

It was at this turning point in history that the common man actually did have democratic opportunities to obtain wealth, security, health, and happiness. A man had the democratic advantage to advance his station in life.

I am not going to begin or include women in this portion of the preface simply because at the beginning development of the United States it was unspoken, but believed that women didn't even have souls. A look at history confirms the female disadvantages. Black Slavery became a political issue. Black male slaves were simply given freedom and the right to vote in 1863. Women did not receive recognition or the right to vote until 1914, fifty one years later. The women had to fight for the right to vote. Slaves didn't fight for that right, others fought for the slaves.

I will also not forget what my Hispanic son in law said during the 2008 election period. He told me that Barrack Obama would win over Hilary Clinton, and then defeat John McCain and Sarah Palin because the people of the United States would choose a man over a woman, even a black man would defeat a woman whether she was black, white, Hispanic, or indigenous. He was so very right and I agreed completely. In a democratic or plutocratic government, it is the male that dominates and possesses the wealth and power.

Democracy began and thrived through the next one hundred years. The plutocratic government of the wealthy, by the wealthy, and for the wealthy didn't like this system very much at all. After the Industrial Revolution, it was determined that the wealthy must take back the government and ruling authority. The elite wealthy didn't like paying 94% of their wealth to a democratic government. The masses needed to pay for the government not them. The plutocrats came back in full force. If anything one must compliment the plutocrats for having patience. The plutocrats set things in motion on a smaller scale, learn from the reactions and set the future for a larger scale, but more carefully planned takeover.

In the late 1920's a crash of Wall Street redistributed the wealth from the workers to the elite plutocrats. This had been tried on a smaller scale in the late 1800's. The financial theft was successful so the elite did it on a larger scale in the 1920's. The wealth funneled down to much fewer elites. The robbery worked well. The plans were formulated for recessions to assist the robbery on smaller but more periodic thefts. The plutocratic elites were planning a global takeover now. There would be a global economic meltdown in the future.

The elite plutocrats determined war was at this time the best offensive. World War I was a bust however; it didn't quite work for them. The plutocrats decided to support socialism financially. Once socialism is established, it is easier to maneuver into a plutocracy, very much like the Bolshevik revolution. The wealthy financed and supported Hitler. The plutocrats manipulated Hitler into place and then began securing the wealth of Germany and Europe. It worked very well indeed.

Franklin Roosevelt became President and established many socialistic reforms that changed tax laws. These revisions put the burden of the government incomes on the working masses. The Internal Revenue Service was created. This separate entity became the federal administrative police for the removal of money from the working masses' pockets. The IRS is quite effective in the terror of intimidation. This entity is not, nor has it ever been legally voted into the Constitution of the United States. Then the government decided to create another entity that is not part of the Constitution of the United States, the Federal Reserve Bank. I define this entity as the exact same banking system established under Nazi Germany to secure and control the wealth of Europe under Hitler and the Nazi Regime. The elite plutocracy of America soon became wealthy financing both sides of World War II. Some of these plutocrats were Henry Ford, Rockefeller, Walker, and Prescott Bush. These men absorbed more of the stolen Jewish and European wealth of World War II.

Democracy wasn't erased entirely though. The United States was still hanging on to freedom, the will, and the power of the people. Labor Unions were strong. The labor unions could not and would not survive in the plutocratic country the elite wealthy envisioned.

After World War II the plan was set in motion to break the labor unions. The marketing was superb. The union leaders were put into positions of wealth and power. The corruption was complete. Then the plutocrats merely had to market this corruption through the mainstream media. The focus was on only a few corrupted unions connected to the criminal mobs. The reality that most unions benefitted both employers and employees was soon lost. The unions were set up to fall apart. The unions were bad guys that stole worker money. The propaganda worked well.

A new media called TV came into the arsenal of the plutocrats. Scientists proved how easily mass markets could now be manipulated. Larger audiences of media blitz could be brainwashed. Slowly the democracy was lured into the hypnosis. Manipulation and media control took control of the American mind quickly and efficiently.

Presidential, Senate, Congressional, State, and local politicians were elected on charisma and TV personality. The Presidents, Senators, and Congressmen were lured into the blackest and most vile of all corruptions. The politicians that were to represent the people slowly succumbed to the seduction of wealth and power. The plutocrats bought them their power and held them to the IOU's. The addiction to power and wealth gave the plutocrats more power, wealth, and control. Laws were made to protect corporate wealth and tax the working masses. The media blitzed the masses with the goodness and rightness of working to help develop and protect the corporate interests.

Unfortunately the Economic enslavement of the American working masses was beginning. I was born into Economic slavery.

Dwight David Eisenhower was one of the last two Presidents in democracy. He warned the American people upon his departure of the changing hands of a government for the people to a government for the corporation. The American public did not listen. The American public bought into the glamour and glitz of media advertising. This was a time of plenty and contentment. It was the time to be happy. There was no place on earth better than America. America has changed in these 250 years from plutocracy to democracy and now oligarchy. Oligarchy is a government influenced by the few. In the case of America those few are the financial, auto, oil, insurance, and retail megalithic corporations.

The time was ripe for oligarchy to take over the rule of the United States. Media manipulation was easier with TV. The corporations chose the candidates and set them up with large amounts of wealth to produce, buy, and advertise a candidate's charisma. It backfired a little in 1959 when a Charismatic JFK won the Presidency. He was wealthy, but he wasn't part of the corporate plan. Nixon was supposed to win.

Kennedy won by the popular vote. The plutocrats quickly fixed that problem by creating the power of the Electoral College. With the Electoral College in place and Kennedy planning to eliminate the greatest plutocratic control of wealth in the United States, The Federal Reserve Bank, it was the time to kill JFK. In November of 1963 JFK was assassinated before he could win a second term.

The Vice President, Lyndon Baines Johnson, was very easily controlled. LBJ was an egotist, boozer, and womanizer. The corporations also used LBJ to push the diversity racial issues. The division of Americans by color was used to push through legislation to weaken democracy with more socialism. A divided identity of Americans with issues of race and color would weaken democratic rule. The plutocrats pushed LBJ into the escalation of the Vietnamese War. Why you ask? It was believed that due to a geologist President, Calvin Coolidge, that there was vast oil off Vietnam. It was a blood for oil war. The plutocrats were now involved in oil. Oil was the gold of the present and the wealth was to be found in oil. Oil was the future wealth and power of the plutocrats. The plans were set to get Nixon in the White House. An oil shortage crisis along with the Vietnam War worked well to get Nixon in since Nixon was anything but charismatic. The plutocrats learned from the charisma ratings by the defeat of Nixon to the charisma of JFK.

Nixon was elected. The Vietnam War had to end. It turned out Vietnam didn't have the oil reserves the plutocrats had believed to be there. Under Nixon the Vietnam War ended. It was time for the plutocrats to focus in on the power and wealth of corporations. Until Nixon health insurance and insurance in general were nonprofit organizations, but as the corporations investigated into insurance programs it was learned that insurance brought in billions but expended only millions. Health insurance was especially lucrative. In 2011 it was revealed that the highest paid CEO was from the insurance industry. This CEO's salary is 156 million dollars a year. The die was cast to regulate payouts of insurance to health care providers under new legislation. This new legislation under President Nixon changed all insurance organizations from non profit to profit. The profits were exponential. This was good for the oligarchy. The value of gold and silver needed to be controlled. The technical invention of the computer also became a weapon in the arsenal of the elite. Gold and precious metals were too scattered and too difficult to maintain safely in the possession of the oligarchy. We changed solid tangible wealth into intangible electronic digits. Nixon removed the gold standard as the financial foundation of currency. It would be easier to erase electronic digits from the masses than to steal a tangible product.

The masses still weren't quite ready to give up democracy yet. Nixon was ousted and the oligarchy couldn't save him. Fortunately TV was not totally controlled by the corporations at this point of time. The manipulations continued in the dark secrets of the corrupted United States Government. The oligarchy couldn't just throw another war. The groomed candidate wasn't ready quite yet.

The corporations deliver the next President to teach the masses what happens when they elect a common man. Jimmy Carter was anything but a common man, but he was presented as such. During the time a strong candidate could have actually defended and protected democracy, the masses were given a weak man with an ego religious problem. Today's world and TV was all about marketing, advertising, and charisma. Carter was doomed to failure by the corporate media. Yet, under Carter's weak presidency, more beneficial legislation for corporations was passed than ever before.

The next President was Ronald Reagan. Here the corporations provided real CHARISMA. Reagan was tall, handsome, looked great in a suit, movie star, and TV personality. Reagan was an image of strength and shoot em at the hip mentality. In fact, Reagan was not qualified for the position in any way means or form. Reagan was easily manipulated by the secret oligarchy behind the Presidential office. The time was at hand to completely crush and destroy the last protection of the working masses. Labor unions were the walking dead. Reagan quickly wielded the axe to strike down the unions once and for all. Reagan was finished. It was time for the chosen candidate, George Herbert Walker Bush. Unfortunately, the Secret Service and FBI was not part of the assassination and by a quirk of fate, Ronald Reagan not only survived the attempt, he recovered from it.

George Herbert Walker Bush, the chosen President of the wealthy and by the wealthy had to wait a little longer to fulfill the return of oligarchy.

George H.W. Bush came sweeping into the Presidential Office to fine tune the oligarchy controls and bring the Asian wealth into the control of the elite wealthy. He did an excellent job. China fell for the banking system hook, line, and sinker. Western idealism swept into the poverty of China like a violent windstorm. Soon communist China fell into the marketed seduction of things just like the Americans and Europeans. Bush and oil, the greatest wealth of the 20th century took over the Middle East. The United States workers known as Fodder to President George H.W. Bush were being sucked deeper into economic slavery as China became the physical slaves of the United States. In exchange, China became the keeper of the gold. The oligarchy didn't really care since wealth was quickly becoming electronic digits. Gold is too hard to manage, maintain, secure, and keep. The United States became the oil guzzling leech of the world. The marketing fed Americans with arrogance of gas guzzling cars, modern appliances, things, things, and more things. America became the policeman of the world under this President. The purpose to police the world was and is to control the world. The test of world policing came with the quick and little war George was given. The power worked in Desert Storm. The time would soon come for a longer and more productive war.

The corporations also know how to divide the nations and this country with partisan prejudice. The elite selectively picked the charismatic Democrat Bill Clinton to be the next President. This was one not a member of the elite, but on the outside skin of the onion. The chosen had started the New World Order, which President George H.W. Bush said quite openly. Another charismatic Democrat was chosen because under Reaganomics and Bush New World Order, the masses realized there was a shifting in the distribution of wealth. Less and less people had more and more wealth. The thieving of wealth was beginning to become more evident. Strategy to bring a brief economic relief to working masses would suffice. Clinton became the President to balance the budget and let the working masses believe their hard work would be rewarded. The oligarchy government was secure. The media marketing blitz worked successfully. The puppet Clinton successfully brought in global economics. The elite obtained more control of global wealth. The time was nearing to obtain it all and successfully enslave the world by economics. The elite wanted to initiate their next phase. They had to discredit the partisan party of Democrats to put in their new Republican puppet. Bill Clinton was attacked on his sexuality. He didn't mind that very much. After all, it wasn't a political scandal. It was a sex scandal. That was a manly thing to deal with. It was macho.

We were led into the Nascar Dad charismatic President, affectionately known as Dubyah. Under Dubyah it was time to reign in complete control of the American Worker. Poppy (George H.W. Bush) and his sons' worked behind the scenes as the Nascar Dad media blitz guffawed and mumbled his way through the Presidency. That was okay since Dick Cheney was the puppeteer, a true oligarch, and put on a great show for the American public. Marvin settled in and sold all American Jobs to foreign countries like China, Indonesia, and India. In these countries, corporate elite oligarchs flourished. Instead of a living wage and middle class economic slaves the corporations had real slavery. The corporate elite oligarchy didn't have to live with a mere 50% to 75% profit. With global slavery the elite now enjoyed 3,000 to 5,000% profit margins. Gluttony is now the common name for corporate profit. Neil Bush entered the internet software markets. In the software markets the most damage could be done to the American economic slave system. The children's education would be controlled and the new generation would be techy, but dumbed down. Banking systems would be easier to control under only a few corporate giants. The health of all Americans would be at insurance company fingertips. Best of all, the new electronic digit wealth of every American could quite easily disappear.

To cover this takeover something had to happen. Fear and terror would work. The elite corporate oligarchy concocted the devastation of a terrorist attack on America. Viola, you have the New York Twin Towers falling. The Financial Center of the United States was attacked. Not only did this bring the fear and terror needed, it was the testing ground for the biggest heist of wealth in the world.

The attack worked. The fear reaction was priceless. The Stock Market crashed and electronic digit wealth disappeared into the catacombs of the Federal Reserve Bank. The people willingly gave up their democratic freedoms to the powerful elite of Washington. Whatever the plutocratic government wanted, was given freely. More power was given to the Presidential office. The corporate lobbyist became the most vital function of American government. Protections went to the corporation of Brown & Root with the name Wackenhut. Our freedoms to travel and live free were removed with airline regulations. Corporations made billions from the destruction of Iraq cities under the guise of War. As we bombed, we gave contracts to corporations to build. We didn't let the American people know we were bombing Iraq for more than a full year before the Twin Towers fell and we declared war.

Industry in the United States came to a screeching halt. Marvin Bush successfully out sourced American jobs and industry to enslaved foreign countries. The United States now offered only service industry low paying wage employment. The crash was coming. The vast majority of wealth in the United States would be in the hands of a few.

The oligarchy would reign in triumph once more and the economic enslavement of the American People would begin in the next election year of 2008.

The brilliant plans of the corporate elite are genius. The elite prepare and finance the puppet they want in control and the economic slaves worship the chosen idol like the golden calf of Moses. The slaves were given golden words of promise and they worshipped the next marketed President. While the division of racial attitudes was being used, the elites crashed the economic system and stole everyone's money from Wall Street. The digits were quickly deposited into the Federal Reserve Bank. The redistribution started instantly in the economic bailouts of the financial industry. The auto industry bailout was merely a red herring to finally destroy the last of the union solidarity. At last the corporate oligarchy owned the wealth and the title to American economic slaves. The large corporations ate the little corporations and the global wealth was neatly placed in elite hands. The media marketed the stupidity of American greed, when in reality we were merely being flogged by the overseer to remind us just who the massah is. The economic slave owns nothing in the reality of oligarchy.

The representatives of the people are puppets of the corporates. Every day more and more laws are being written to economically enslave Americans. These laws are presented to benefit the people. In Reality the laws benefit only the ruling elite. An example is the first bill made into Law under the Obama Administration, equal pay and equal rights for women. The law states that an employee can now file legal suits 120 days after termination in any discrimination of age, pay, etc. Women can file harassment law suits, inequity of pay, and hostile environment suits after termination. What the media didn't release was the fact this law was after Obama and the other representatives changed a previous law allowing this legal suit to be brought before a local judiciary, or state judiciary. The law was changed to provide for the legal suit to be brought before a Federal Justice. I ask, who the HELL could afford a Federal Attorney and file a Federal Suit? A terminated employee can't afford a cheap sleazy lawyer, much less a Federal Attorney. Did anyone analyze the cost difference between a local judiciary cost and Federal judiciary cost?

Another law extolled by the media was the consumer protection act signed by President Obama. This was pushed through the corporate puppets of the Congress to protect Consumers. The only significant difference of the entire bill for Consumers was that instead of 30 days notice to raise interest, the credit holder now must give a 45 day notice to raise interest rates. To protect financial entities from consumer bankruptcy, many big ticket items can no longer be purchased on credit. There is a restriction on minimum ticket purchases. The worst part of this new law is that prior to it, a limit of 33% interest rate for creditors to charge has been removed. Creditors no longer have a cap on interest charges. Creditors can raise rates to 100% if they choose, and they will in the future until the backs of the economic slaves are broken and there is nothing but bone left.

The economic slaves are fed polished shiny apples that contain bitter and murderous poison. We devour it as the starving in our false belief in the idols presented to us.

Who is the oligarchy? They are a group of people that have been in existence since mankind began trading. They have many names, the Bilderberg Group, Illuminati, Dutch Trading Company, the Twelve, the Freemasons, and other names. There are many names, but the reality is that it is a group of men, yes men. Women are not allowed other than the outside of the onion skin. This group controls and dominates all wealth in the world. The group also decrees exactly what wealth is defined as. The powerful oligarchy has been nearly destroyed many times in ancient and past history by kings when the group became more powerful than the king, but they return each time more powerful than the previous incarnation.

The group of elite do consider themselves far superior to the common man. The sole purpose of the common man is to serve them. They are the Gods of ancient Greece. And the current 2012 Presidential Candidates are examples of the Caesars of Ancient Rome just before the FALL OF ROME. Ergo, they are all insane, corrupted, and greedy, megalomaniacs funded and controlled by the oligarchy.

CONTENTS

The Hemingses of Monticello

Current economic enslavement of the American workforce parallel

A new form of enslavement has appeared in the 21st Century. It has been a long time returning since the 1860 emancipation, but after political movement, buyoffs, and economic controls the American worker has completely become enslaved to the corporations.

I would first like to explain my perception of slavery with the Hemingses of Monticello.

This wonderful book delved into not only in the history of Thomas Jefferson and an affair with a slave, Sally Hemings, but the anthropological study of slavery during the time period of the American Revolution. This book studied a slave family in a scientific manner including the social customs, environment, philosophy, and politics of the time. Here is where I start to draw the parallels of the current 21st century enslavement.

The Hemingses of Monticello revolves around the Hemings slave family during pre Revolutionary War, the Revolutionary War, and Post Revolutionary war. The author's study of this period is enlightening and informative about the economics of slavery as well as the contradictory social mores and customs of enslavement.

During the Sally Hemings time period it was factual that no one born into slavery could rise to complete freedom. Slaves were considered chattel, fodder, and property. Slaves were given no rights or opportunities. Slaves were born to work for the wealthy and became a part of the owner's legal property. There is no difference in this time period. You are born into economic slavery without any escape from it. Many people tout that they are not controlled by any debt or credit difficulties. These people fool themselves. Anyone in this society that is not independently wealthy and does not have to work for a living is an economic slave. Your job is at the will of the employer. Many retail corporations, federal government, state government, and other employers write this clause into the employee handbooks. The clause is that employment is by the will of the employer. I ask you, is this any different from a slave owner having the right to buy and sell a slave as property? We are allowed to work in certain places at certain times by the benevolence of the employer. If you are no longer of any viable interest to the owner, you are thrown out to fend for yourself. Corporations are bought and sold. These new corporations buy and sell the workers. The old corporation sells you to the new corporation with new rules, wages, and agendas. You have no say in the selling of the corporation. If the new corporation doesn't like you because of age, race, or sex, you are thrown out. Is that any different from the selling of plantations in the Antebellum Period? No, it is not. Your options as a non-functioning slave due to illness, disease, age, or downsizing of the business is charity from family, friends, or churches. If these charities are not available, you have the options of becoming homeless and hopefully dying quickly. The slave owner may have offered benefits, retirement, or other programs, but due to the owner's economic mindset and situation, those options can quickly be rescinded.

The Hemings slaves worked in the house or light labor work at the benevolence of Thomas Jefferson. When age, disease, or downsizing of the plantation occurred the slave was sold to another slave owner, lived on the charity of family, or retirement on the benevolence of the slave owner. In this case the slave owner was the plutocrat Thomas Jefferson.

Slaves were bought and sold solely for economic purpose. Slaves did own limited personal positions which could be confiscated as legal property of the owner at will. Slaves were allowed to live in slave houses or private shanties on the owner's property, but at the will of the owner. The owner could rescind any lodging at anytime.

Here is the first parallel to the 21st century economic slave. The 21st century worker has literally been called Fodder by President George Herbert Walker Bush. Financial Institutions buy and sell our property at will. A house you believe you own can be foreclosed at the will of the lender. A lender, or the true owner, can raise your rent by interest levels that completely bankrupts your income or slave wage. Your property is sold to another owner and you become the chattel of that new owner. The new owner can sell you at will to another financial lender. Like the Hemings slave, you are bought and sold at the will of the owner and have no voice in where or which owner takes possession. That big beautiful car you now own is no different than a mule or horse owned during the Hemings time period. That car or animal really belongs to the owner who can at will take possession at any time and sell it to another owner. The Revolutionary slave had the options to use the animal for work, but the owner put many restrictions on the use. A slave could not venture far without owner consent. A slave had to carry papers from the owner showing the true ownership. Have a good laugh with me now. The car driver has the right to use the vehicle for work, but there are limits to usage of the vehicle. The actual economic owner, usually a bank, demands that paper work be carried to prove true ownership and the driver is responsible financially for that vehicle. We call our new papers, insurance policies giving money to the economic owner should something happen to the vehicle. Like the slave patrols, the police of the 21st century check these papers carefully and the economic slave must have them in possession. The State government requires registration on the vehicle, and the writ of a driver's license to prove you can drive. How different is that from the papers a slave held to prove the slave had the right to move about. It is also a method to keep track of the slave. The Federal Government has come up with a method of tracking and marking the slave. It is called the IRS. Any economic slave in the United States is given a social security number. No one is allowed to work in this country without a number. No one can drive a vehicle, get a driver's license, attend school or college, rent a home, see a doctor, see a dentist, etc without the precious economic slave number of the social security. At one time a number wasn't needed until an American reached the age of 18 or began to work, or drove a car. Like the days of the old slaves, a child born must be given an identity to be marked as an economic slave.

Similarly, the economic slave is at the will of the economic owner with the vehicle. Should the economic slave default in any way to the owner, the owner can at will take possession of the vehicle. During the slave periods, any and all possessions of a slave were and became property of the slave owner. If a slave hatched a chicken, trained a falcon, grew vegetables, or whatever, that property could be taken by the slave owner as its right of property.

Like the comedian said, "Nothing has changed."

The slave during the time of Thomas Jefferson had one purpose. This purpose was to work for the master and provide the master a comfortable prosperous life. A slave was not allowed to benefit from any of the master's luxuries or profits. A slave was allowed the necessities to live and function.

Do you see the parallel here?

As economic slaves we work for the business. This business may be for corporations, governments, or small companies. The small companies are quickly disappearing though. We are given the basics of food, shelter, transportation, and clothing. Some of us work the fields. Some of us are given the opportunity to work in the master's house, but we are not allowed to enjoy the benefits of luxury and lifestyles. When we forget our place in the scope of the corporation hierarchy, we are quickly put back in our place.

Just like the great masters, there are the overseers that also have a place in the hierarchy that remind you of your place. In the world today, the overseers are known as managers. These managers are hired by the corporations to keep the slaves in line and out of their sight and mind. A master truly does not want to mingle with lower beings. The master wants the work done without dealing at all with the workforce.

The corporations just like Thomas Jefferson put on the false face of their benevolence and kindness. The corporation lauds the cheering it receives when the CEO, COO, or whatever acronym fits the master by its workforce. Truly they speak of being good, kind, and benevolent to their workforce. The manager's are instructed to make us happy with motions like cheers in a high school pep rally or small monetary blessings at holidays.

Like Jefferson who bragged that he trained his slaves to be better, they boast of education, health, and benefit packages. Like Jefferson, the corporations write pretty words on documents befriending slaves. Every Major Corporation, company, institution, or government has pretty words of a handbook that defines rights and obligations of the worker.

The reality of the pretty words is that the slave owner or corporation leaves vacant holes and ambiguity for the overseers or managers to do as they will to the workers. When the manager abuses the worker, there isn't any more recourse for the worker than the slave. The corporation does not interfere with the lower operations a manager deems best.

Thomas Jefferson touted consistently his abhorrence to slavery. Thomas Jefferson claimed to be benevolent to his slaves. History portrays him as being kind and generous to his slaves. History portrays Thomas Jefferson as educating his slaves. The reality was that Thomas Jefferson never once interfered or objected to any of his overseers raping a slave woman or girl. He did not interfere or object to his overseers using violence on his slaves both men and women. Slaves under Thomas Jefferson were beaten and whipped sometimes to death. Thomas Jefferson's overseers raped slave women and girls and created more slaves by such rapes. Thomas Jefferson only educated his house slaves or the fair skinned slaves that he considered of higher intelligence due to their skin color. Even those slaves were merely educated in the higher opportunities of skilled trades. Thomas Jefferson's slaves were never educated in the higher learning such as philosophy, psychology, astronomy, or sciences. The field slaves of darker skin endured the whippings, rapes, and cruelty of the overseer without any interference of the great master.

It is the same with corporations today. The CEO or Executive sits in the great house and enjoys all of the luxury, wealth, and elite lifestyle provided by the worker force of his economic slaves. Between the Executive and the worker are the managers, mid managers, and supervisors. These managers abuse, berate, and sometimes use workers for their own pleasures, whatever that pleasure may be. These managers set schedules, work, and time tables based upon their ideals to the great Executive. These managers are allowed to interpret in any way the directions of the Executive without fear of interference or reprisals by the Executives.

There are those who claim they have crawled up from the ghetto to live the American dream. They claim Americans have the opportunity to break free from imposed slavery. This is true if you are a greedy sports star and rock star with a market manager, drug lord, or white collar criminal. Perhaps you slept with an official or your daddy is rich. Or one has to be favored with financial banking to get anywhere in the world today. Beyond the aforementioned lifestyles, it is impossible to break free of the economic slavery. Actually the lifestyles of the rich and famous are nefarious anyway. They can be at the top, but tweak the wrong elitist and Humpty Dumpty will soon come tumbling down.

WHAT REALLY GOES ON "UNDER THE APRON"

Customer Abuse

Unless you have worked retail sales under large corporate management you will never comprehend the abuse from both customers and management.

The corporations now call floor sales representatives associates. The change in terms removes the sales stigma from the corporation. If there are sales representatives or sales forces, the corporation would have the definition requiring proper compensation for any sales generated. Commissions would need to be considered. That would require compensation which would cut into the corporate profit. The corporations change the title to associates, or floor associates because it sounds like we are all one big happy family working together for the benefit of both.

Nothing could be further from the truth. With the change of terms to associate, the corporation no longer is required to compensate for sales generated. The corporations obtain a benevolent image and retain all profits. The associate is paid above minimum wage without benefit of commissions under sales remuneration.

The corporation maintains a benevolent image while on the floor, or the front lines, an associate must endure verbal abuse from customers and managers. There are times there is physical abuse from customers.

I have personally encountered a few of these in retail corporations. One woman grabbed my collar and started shaking me violently because I didn't fold a dress properly in the bag and packed other items she had purchased with the dress. I recall an older woman coming through the checkout line with her granddaughter. She said to the child, "You see, if you don't go to college you'll end up with a job like this for the uneducated." That was verbal abuse and cut to my heart. I have a degree and nearly all the people I worked with in the retail store did. Many were teachers earning money to finish higher degrees, or supplementing summer incomes. Many were college students working their way through college. Just recently, a Hispanic man grabbed and shook me, bruising my arm because I did not speak Spanish and couldn't understand what he wanted, nor could he understand my questions although I was trying to assist him and take him to the service desk to get a Spanish speaking floor associate.

It is a joke among associates to stay away from certain locations. These locations have extremely heavy items that need to be moved onto a freight cart or shopping cart. While some of the items are so heavy that only a piece of machinery can move it, the biggest problem is that most of the items can be moved by a person to a freight or shopping cart, they are just a bit heavy like mulch, concrete, sand, litter, fertilizer, and soil bags. The customer may need at least assistance to lift the object. Instead the customer attitude is that you are his economic slave. He is a visiting plantation owner and you must serve him to his satisfaction. That means the associate has in many instances had to lift the heavy object alone, call for help to help the associate (even though the customer and associate could have done it together), and sometimes in pouring rain, sleet, and or snow, load the object into the transporting vehicle while the customer remains sheltered and protected from elements.

Abuse from Customers' Children

Young children run rampant in retail stores. Parents think they are cute, or too occupied on their cell phone conversations to notice their child is destructive to store property or are in danger of hurting themselves. When an associate quietly and gently warns or reprimands the child, the parent suddenly becomes a blood seeking demon that screams obscenities at the associate. The customer then reports the incident to the assistant manager, who in turn reprimands the associate for terrible customer service or gives the associate a written reprimand. I have known associates that were fired because they dared to actually restrain a child from being hurt or hurt others. The parents were furious that the man touched their child. Parents are just a furious for a verbal comment from an associate when the child in fact does endanger not only their person, but others as well.

In one case a child was using a plastic baseball bat and slamming it forcefully on a Christmas Display. The parents did nothing. I knew if I said anything I would be reprimanded or written up. If the display was damaged, that didn't matter. I waited until finally the child pulled out an empty box that held the display and crawled inside. The parents were completely oblivious the entire time and started walking away. I walked past them and commented politely, "Don't forget your merchandise." I pointed to the moving box their child was in.

Another child incident occurred when I spoke to three children using a flat cart handle as a jungle gym. If one of those flat carts would flip on top of a child, the child could be seriously injured or killed. The warning to parents about the dangers of children riding carts and flat carts is run on a consistent basis in the retail stores. The warnings are simply noise background and completely ignored by most parents. When I spoke to the children and asked them to cease, I was immediately called to task by the mother and told to mind my "F.....G" business. She continued with a tirade of expletives that could curl your hair. I walked away. It was nearly a half hour later when the mother cornered me once more and shot off another tirade of expletives at me. Wow, I never again tried to warn a parent or child again. I figured if the parents didn't care if their children were hurt or maimed, maybe I shouldn't worry about it. I didn't want to get myself in trouble or lose my job, which I do need financially, because a parent complained to a manager about my interference. Employees have been fired for such things, whether the employee was right in the correction is not a relevant factor. The only factor that matters is that the employee upset a customer. Oh yes, employees have been fired for protecting children. One employee I know physically restrained a child in the building material section. The child could have been hurt with various implements he had picked up and was recklessly swinging around. The child could have hurt others. The parents were not in the immediate area. An employee told the boy to put the equipment down. The boy swore at the employee and laughed at him. The employee then grabbed the boy by his shirt and told him firmly to put down the equipment. The boy dropped the equipment and ran to his parents sobbing. The parents immediately took their precious darling to a manager and told the manager their boy was shaken up because this big bad mean associate had grabbed him and yelled at him. The parents told the manager no associate has the right to touch their darling child. The employee was fired.

Children often show complete disrespect for associates. Like their parents and peers, the person that works in retail stores is a target for their abuse. I have been so frequently insulted by children, it is difficult to remember all the insults and slurs. My personality doesn't allow me to shrug it off. It hurts deeply. Just recently a four or five year old boy was telling his father where to go and what to do. I was waiting patiently to get through the aisle. The father requested quietly and politely, "Please move and sit down." The child looked at me and said, "Why? She's just an old lady." I had another four year old girl literally push me and looked up at me with such venom I thought I was staring into the eyes of rattlesnake that just woke up from hibernation. Her parents were with her. I looked at them and saw the same venomous and contemptuous glare. No, I wasn't in their way. The girl just wanted more room to walk three abreast down the aisle.

Associates must endure any and all customers that are having a bad day, a fight with the spouse, not feeling well, or any excuse that requires a whipping boy. Silently we are forced to endure cursing, anger, prejudice, sexual discrimination, shouting, harassment, and stubborn self involved egotists that truly believe the world revolves around them. They insist their wants be satisfied instantly and you must fulfill the want this instant want or you are not providing customer service.

It isn't funny at all when as an associate you must endure the rage, anger, and verbal abuse of a customer. The purpose of the customer is to demean you as a person to feel better. There isn't anything one can do to appease these customers since they do not want to be appeased. These customers simply want to demean and hurt you because they are hurting or feeling bad. And they can. It doesn't matter if they should demean a worker. It only matters that customers can demean workers. Remind you of the antebellum slavery period? The slaves had to put up with all any abuse of the owners or visitors.

The intimidations and abuse by customers could be a log book of several thousand pages for just one store including all departments in just one month.

Unfortunately once that anger is unleashed on the associate; the personality of the customer changes when a manager is called. The horrendously rude angry customer turns into a little puppy complaining the associate was rude, obnoxious, or not helpful. The manager sees this nice person complaining about service. Guess what happens? The associate is convicted, hung, and quartered without trial or defense.

What is the psychology of the sudden change of personality when the manager appears? First of all, the associate is unconsciously the customer's servant. The customer has complete and total control of the servant. The servant is theirs to abuse as they will. The manager is at a higher level; therefore it is no longer the servant. The manager becomes the equal or superior and the whole psychology changes.

Speaking of puppies, the store rule is no animals in the store. Customers bring their pets in all the time. One had a cart full of small dogs. The dogs peed on the floor. Guess who had to mop up the dog pee from the floor?

I see this as a similar situation during the Antebellum Slavery time period. A visitor to the plantation has a bad day, verbally abuses the slave, and when he sees the master he complains about the rude servant simply because the slave didn't bow low enough for his satisfaction, or jump high enough when he said jump. The master becomes upset with the slave. The overseer or manager is told of the incident and then promptly beats the slave. The slave of course wasn't even given the thought or questioned what happened. The slave was simply beaten. And don't kid yourself. In reality any manager, supervisor, or mid manager could and would beat an associate if it wasn't currently against the law. If caning or whipping were legal, we the corporate worker in the corporate world of the 21st Century would be caned whipped, or flogged on a daily basis. The sadistic side of corporate management would love to set examples and enhance the fear.

Management Abuse

In fact, the psychology of most managers and mid managers in retail corporate America is that of overseer to the economic slaves. The corporation is similar to Thomas Jefferson and his enslaved plantation. They all project the image of benevolence, but do not inhibit abuse of the slaves by the managers. The corporations remain benevolent in the public and should something horrendous come to light, the corporations quickly claim "Plausible Deniability" or "That wasn't reported to us. We have no knowledge of such incidents." The corporation is removed quickly from any legal or moral responsibility to their employees with such escape route rhetoric. These are entrapments for the associate for they are quickly labeled as a disgruntled employee. The corporation is always the innocent and the employee is always bad, greedy, and or inferior.

One such plausible deniability occurred a few years ago. Within a major corporation, a young woman, a 16 year old was consistently sexually abused by a manager. The young woman had to immediately respond to the manager's need for coitus at any given time. If the cell phone rang and he wanted her for coitus, she had to respond immediately wherever and whenever the male manager wanted. The young woman was told her job depended on keeping him pleased. She of course needed this job. The young woman didn't know what to do or how to stop it. Finally her mother found out. Her mother contacted an attorney and the Corporation was quickly and publically informed. Does it take the news media or a law suit to bring such abuse to the attention of the corporation? Of course the corporation denied knowledge of any such happenings in their wonderland, benevolent, and employee Friendly Corporation.

The corporation quickly moved the manager to another franchise. Instead of removal, the corporation basically promoted the man. To the employees like me, it was a message to send him for fresh meat. It dumbfounded me that the manager's employment was not terminated and the manager was not arrested for statutory rape, since the employee was under the age of 18. The law is clear about sexual relations with a child under the age of 18. The corporation obviously bought off the city and police to keep things quiet and get the media off their Nirvana Corporation. Such a trial would be media meat and detrimental to their public image. The mother learned of it and felt her daughter's mental anguish was not properly remediated. The mother pursued and filed a law suit against the corporation. The Corporation quickly decried "Plausible Deniability." Since there is no more information on the news, the lawyer and mother were most likely were paid off with vast sums of money. Thus the corporation once again lives in their wonderland Nirvana of the benevolent corporation. I seriously doubt this corporation did anything or changed anything that would prevent this from happening again.

A TV program began in 2010 called "Undercover Boss". It was a delightful program of entertainment genre, because the smaller corporation's CEO would go undercover and actually work within the company or corporation he managed. Leaving the small Ivory Tower and working with the peasants was an eye opener for the CEO's and things were changed after their experiences. Hooter's CEO found sexual harassment in one location and an over achieving female in another. In Waste Management, the CEO discovered sexual discrimination and a power controlling bullying mid manager. Yes, things were changed. It was fun for me to watch the Ivory Tower men working the trenches. Imagine the better behavior of the managers knowing they were being videotaped. What would have gone on if there weren't cameras rolling? Unfortunately, these were small corporate CEO's compared to the behemoth corporations. The abuse continues without a thought of anyone in the ivory towers thinking "Does this go on everywhere?" Not one of the behemoth corporations would consider a bill of rights for employees. There are only rules regarding management demands, and nothing written for the employees in a handbook. The corporations deny unions to enter the world of the employees with threat, horror stories, and lies about unions as if they were all bad. Instead the corporations offer more rhetoric and buzz words of their benevolence. The unions could actually provide a balance to rules and regulations for the employee and the corporation. Such a working arrangement would be advantageous and provide a happy and content workforce. Corporations however, have no interests in happy employees. The mindset of the corporations is that of slave owner over slaves. The workforce are not people, the work force are ignorant fodder at the command and desire of the corporation. The economic slaves continue to be the victims of master mindset and power. What a country this could be if corporations did care and invest in their employees.

I still believe that corporations could truly work at creating harmonious work environments if they wanted and thus, unions would truly not be necessary.

CEO's and all Upper Management have little reality of actual front line encounters and abuse from managers and customers. Upper Management levels surround themselves with the yes people, the arse kissers, the buzz words and rhetoric. It is very difficult to understand front line reality when people surrounding you tell you how wonderful you are and jump to preen your ego. The vast separation between the Ivory Tower and front lines is the difference between a heaven and a hell.

Unfortunately for the arse kissers and yes people, they will be the first to be sacrificed if right or justice nears. I have seen those employees thrown to the wolves if reporters (there are very few of true reporters left) start sniffing around legal issues.

Why the discrepancy? It is similar to a 'pass the words on' game. By the time any rule has been passed down through upper level management, to mid management, to supervisors, and reaching the employee, the rule has been completely misinterpreted, damaged, and skewed dramatically. There is also the fact that anything coming from the corporate level is interpreted as an edict. The interpretations are never reviewed or investigated by the Corporation's Top Management. This lack of follow up is similar to the Thomas Jefferson Plantation Master Syndrome. The master never investigated if his rules were skewed and turned into abuse by the overseers. A slave could never approach the master with such allegations. The master trusted the overseer was carrying out instructions and the work was accomplished. There was never a need to see just how the overseer achieved the instructions. The slave had no escape or hope of ever approaching the master for fair or just treatment. The slave is the slave and the lowest ignorant in the pecking order of humanity or corporations.

An employee likewise could never approach the corporation with questions regarding the treatment of employees by management.

In corporation rules or handbooks for retail employees the responsibility slants heavily on the employee. The handbooks require employees to follow ethics, codes, rules, and regulations. There are few and quite vague rules for management. In one particular employee handbook there are **11** pages of rules for employees and a small paragraph for management. The management is allowed in this paragraph to create rules for the efficient running of the store. The key word empowering intimidation and bullying in these handbooks is "managerial discretion".

In a corporate store it is not unusual to hear managers and supervisors yell or snap at employees. A young man I know working at a mega corporate store as a cashier asked a question regarding a duty he was not certain of. The manager snapped at him and spoke to him as an errant child with anger. The young man is not quite 20. If anyone believes that corporations care, especially mega corporations, I say bless you and hope you still believe (I do believe. I do believe. Keep saying it, it becomes your truth.) There might be rare managers and rare cases of caring, but I haven't seen or heard of them from any of the people I know in mega corporate retail environments. In one retail store an armed robbery occurred recently. The young male cashier, a college student, was completely shaken up. To my knowledge, the only thing done for the young man was permission to take a few days off when he simply could not go back to work or be expected to work the next day. I know of the funeral of an old long time employee of a mega corporation where his immediate manager did not even show up at the memorial. The store manager did not make an appearance either, there were no donations for the family other than money from other employees. However, when a spouse of a manager died, all the managers gathered money, food, and supplies for the manager's home and family. All the managers including the store manager took time away from the store on company time to help with arrangements for the service. It reminded me of the story of Thomas Jefferson and Sally Hemings. Sally's daughter, Thomas Jefferson's daughter, died. The infant's burial was attended by the slave family, Thomas Jefferson did not attend. His daughter was buried in the slave plots. When Thomas Jefferson lost his youngest daughter from his first marriage, there was a big funeral and burial. We know why of course, his youngest daughter from his first marriage was white. The infant daughter was born of a slave. While there are and always will be inequity, some of the inequity just shouldn't be.

Here are some examples of rules these managers put in place, not specified by a corporate rule. The identifier of the store must be worn when clocking in or clocking out. In the case of a store, the location of the store identifier in a locker and the time clock are about 4 minutes apart including the opening of the locker, retrieving the identifier, and walking to the time clock. The walk to the time clock is through the retail store. Customers do approach employees for information and help even if they are not clocked in yet. The customer does not appreciate being told they need to wait a moment until the employee is clocked in. The retail store obtains a total of 16 free minutes from the employee for the day with this practice. Many of my co-employees actually received formal disciplinary write ups for this offense. It didn't matter that the employee would have been late, and summarily receive a written disciplinary action for that offense since at the time of this incident there was a 2 minute rule. An associate could not clock in more than 2 minutes before or 2 minutes after. If this occurred the associate would receive a written disciplinary action.

Fortunately another retail corporation enforced such a rule and the employees filed suit against the corporation and won. I am certain the corporate headquarters was not aware of what was happening in this retail store. When the news broke about the employees winning the law suit, the management in the store stopped enforcing their rule with written disciplinary actions. Unfortunately the practice is still in place in a particular store with managerial comments if the employee is not wearing a store identifier when clocking in. If the manager or supervisor is in a bad mood that day, they may verbally reprimand an employee for the identifier infraction.

It is fortunate that employees won the lawsuit, but the practices still continue without a paper trail to verify the hostile environment. It also allows management and supervisors to harass employees they do not like or just need a whipping boy that day to relieve their frustrations.

One of my favorite ridiculous fear intended hostile environment rules in a store was the minute before and two minute after clock in shift rule. Any employee that clocked in 1 minute prior to their scheduled time or two minutes after their scheduled time received a written disciplinary action. Employees had to wait in the time clock lines to punch in. Everyone waited until the 1 minute before time. Within those precious seconds associates did manage to clock in, but many times the clock did not have time to adjust for a new punch. This meant miss punches.

When there is a miss punch the employee has to get a signed waiver from the management. The employee never knows there is a miss punch until clocking in the next day. The employee then must find a manager, which is quite difficult to do. After a search for the manager and obtaining the management signature, the employee turns in the signed waiver to a special room. The employee calls up the computer person or manager to release the employee from a time clock freeze. This is usually another few minutes, and in our case a very grumpy and unfriendly computer employee enters the release after yelling and complaining about you to you. The employee is now clocking in 20 to 30 minutes late for shift. This causes another written disciplinary action against the employee. The employees have learned to take 2 release forms with them for signature. One release form is for the miss punch and the other is for clocking in late.

Many co-workers in a store received written disciplinary actions for such a crime of miss punch although the fault was too many employees clocking in at the one minute before and the time clock could not reset itself for the next employee. This was never a written rule. Although the management never scribed the rule for written documentation the employees still received disciplinary actions. Word of mouth spread quickly, and soon the economic slaves were in proper behavior patterns and making certain that the corporate retail store received not one minute excess in non work time pay.

Of course there are exceptions to the rule based upon the disparity of some employees over others. There are some special chosen employees that do as they will without worry of management enforcement of rules. Disparity is and always will be part of employment.

Clocking in on time is another difficulty with retail corporations. We are responsible adults and do make every effort to be on time. We as responsible adults work because we need the income. We also care for our fellow co-workers and realize our presence is required for the flow of their work hours. We realize that if we are late, our co-workers would be alone on the floor and overwhelmed. A cashier is exhausted standing for 2 straight hours and needs that 15 minute respite. If you are not there to relieve that cashier for break, we know that cashier is miserable. We also know that if we are late we will mess up the break and lunch times. We as fellow workers do appreciate the extra burden or missed breaks and lunches. We don't need management threatening us when we respect and understand our co-workers needs. Sadly, all of the above ridiculous rules were inflicted upon workers by different managers.

It is understandable that management does have difficulties with employees that exhibit habitual patterns of tardiness. I have noted that instead of addressing the pattern with employees, managers and supervisors create new verbal rules. These verbal rules are enforced to the mass instead of the individual. All suffer for the few. The managers do not really manage at all, and quite simply, do not want to deal with confrontation. Because of this lack of managerial training and human resource departments a person that rarely if ever clocks in late receives the same written disciplinary action the chronic late punch employee receives. This inequity is to be used as a warning to the employee that shows a chronic late pattern. All are punished.

The psychology of punishing all for the few is supposed to put guilt on the chronically late employee. Generally the habitually late employee doesn't think about the punishment for all. The reality of the situation is that it creates anger and hostility from the good employees. The environment in the retail store becomes more of a hostile and fear management environment.

Another target of management punishing all for the few is the habitual call out employee. These employees have consistent crisis and or illnesses. Weekend call outs are always the highest because most employees outside of retail stores have the week end off. Spouses have a need to spend time with their family, and the weekend is that time. Young people like to party on weekends and many times aren't quite sober enough to drive their cars to work, much less put in a full day at work. Some management believes that anyone calling out on a weekend should receive a written disciplinary action.

One Corporate handbook says written disciplinary actions require a consistent pattern of violations. I have rarely seen the employee with consistent patterns receive written violations. As stated previously, the entire workforce suffers under a new and oppressive rule. It is also noted that many times the habitual violating employee receives recognition awards such as employee of the month. It has been related that this positive award would make the employee make more of an effort to better. I have yet to see this reverse psychology work. I note that the reverse psychology generally antagonizes the general workforce. The usual result is the good employee feels it isn't as necessary to work hard to be recognized. The employee feels as though bad behavior is rewarded, why show good behavior?

It is even more difficult for people that only work weekends. "When could an employee call out?" When an employee only works weekends because it is a second job and one hopes others get a week end day off because of a need to work. If that weekend person calls out sick, they are generally really ill. The employee shouldn't have to come up with a medical excuse signed by a doctor after they have received a written disciplinary action. Even if the employee provided a written medical excuse signed by a doctor, would that guarantee the removal of the disciplinary action? What Doctor's office is open on a weekend? If you are sick, you could go to a walk in clinic and to be prepared with an excuse. If you are sick, isn't it a better plan to keep that illness quarantined and get plenty of rest. Even a party now and then is understandable. The written disciplinary action should only be used as a last resort for habitual and chronic patterns in work related irresponsibility by the employee, but generally it isn't.

As an employee, I have rarely seen habitual and chronic patterns punished. Usually all suffer for the few. It is difficult when you are ill, need to call out, and you have only called out sick once in the year but are afraid of a write up. It is aggravating to an associate that doesn't abuse the rules to suffer with the few that abuse the rules.

The morale isn't high in work places where there isn't good management of staff. When morale is low, illness is rampant. The unhappier the workforce, the higher the sick list will be. Corporations have long forgotten this simple fact. Regrettably the American workplace today in general does not have good management. In the place of qualified management are primarily men with a few women that pretend or honestly surrender their souls to the corporation, and who are good with jumbling, fiddling, and making numbers show corporations good things.

Human Resources once had a good and solid open door for employees, which have turned into the monster perpetuating the importance of their job. Human Resources turned itself into a revolving door for employees. As long as employees need to be hired, they had a job. Even this dark side of Human Resources has disappeared. Human Resource is now internet faced. The information is handled by an internet technology guy that turns it over to number crunchers. There are no more human to human communications in the workforce. We are no longer people. We are crunched numbers. We have no protection as individuals. Can we understand how the Corporation views the employees? We are nothing. We are without right to think, eat, or live comfortably. We are only here to breed more calves for slaughter. Is this not a description of an economic slave? Does this remind you of the Antebellum Slavery Era?

There lies another of the great issues of American retail stores. The management does not know how to manage.

Management in corporations function, they do not manage. The retail managers respond and function to corporate edicts, marketing plans, sales goals, everyday minor crisis, and purchases. The managers disregard input from front line employees. The corporations are so large and so full of themselves, they only want functioning robots. Local management mirrors that largesse. That is why the associate is must sell inventory for a product year round when it should only be used twice a year in the locale with threat of sanctions. The corporate buyers make the deals. The front line workers must sell the deals.

Managers are not hired to manage so therefore no management skills are necessary. The corporate retailer wants bean counters to creatively balance their choices. If a person has skills in managing hours to balance sales, the corporation is happy. If a person has skills to place purchases including the skill to stuff 10 pounds of shit into a 5 pound bag, the corporation is happy.

Corporate Abuse

The most insidious of abuse is that from the Corporation itself. The corporation is blindsided by their firm belief in their benevolence, rhetoric, and buzz words. Yes, they really believe in their goodness. Just like Thomas Jefferson who truly believed he was a good, kind, and intelligent man. Yet like Thomas Jefferson they do not see the havoc and unfair practices their benevolence creates. Just like Thomas Jefferson they do not understand the reactions to their actions. The corporate executives never ask, walk, or talk to the field hands. The Corporate Executives maintain their pristine life style in their ivory towers. The Corporate Executives never work the fields or deal on a day to day basis in the fields or the front lines. The Corporate Executives never feel the hand or whip of the overseers or managers. If any cruelty is reported, it is quickly covered up, buried, ignored, or excused with the cry of plausible deniability. Surely nothing bad happens, ever! Surely our field hands are treated gently and kindly because we are gentle and kind.

YEAH RIGHT!

The corporate executives see what they choose to see. The corporate executives decry the truth as an offense.

In many ways I agree with executives that laugh at truth, because in fact truth is not definable. Truth is easily tossed in the corporate garbage cans because truth is perception by an individual. If the corporations do not perceive the situation or incident as truth, it is not.

Corporations will never seek facts in a situation or incident. The corporations do not perceive the situation or incident, so there is no need for fact. Fact seeking is an art that has been long lost in Executive Ivory Towers. The Ivory Towers will ignore the unhappy faces, the pain, and hardships their edicts cause.

Here is an example of such investigations when an employee reports an incident: An assistant manager loudly, verbally, and angrily reprimanded employees in front of customers. Another employee reported the incident to the employee hot line that is supposed to be anonymous. A week later the employee that reported the incident was called into the office by a human relations employee contacted by corporate. It was instantly realized from the reporting employee that HR had determined by investigation just who reported the incident.

The conversation with the guilty employee, the one that reported the incident anonymously, indicated that within the prior week the incident was not investigated, but interrogations were made to determine just who placed the call. The employee was asked why the call was placed. The employee remarked that the public shouting at employees was a violation of the respect value of the corporation and on a managerial level such an act was not only inappropriate but humiliating and disrespectful to the employees. To this employee's principles, if a reprimand is required it is to be done in a positive, not negative, and private atmosphere. That would be respectful.

To the employee's surprise, the HR stated nothing about the inappropriateness of a screaming manager in public, in sight and hearing of not only adult customers but children present as well. (And we wonder where our children learn bullying?) Instead the HR stated that since no customers complained about the incident and a customer did not write about the incident there didn't seem to be any problem.

The HR then asked the employee why the incident was personally upsetting, since the employees shouted at said they were wrong. The HR asked what the employee thought should be done about the manager.

The employee was too stunned for words. The employee realized that management did not see any issue with a manager shouting angrily at employees in front of customers. The employee replied that the manager should have a positive discussion with the assistant manager to aide in understanding the value of respect, dignity, and proper methods of necessary, not arbitrary reprimand if required.

To the employee's shock, the HR again stated that the employees stated they were in the wrong and since no customer's complained, there wasn't any problem.

The employee left with the following remark, "The issue isn't an individual person or personality. The issue wasn't the right or wrong of an employee action or reaction. The issue was a corporate value. More time needed to be spent on understanding the issue."

The employee also learned that there was no such thing as an anonymous employee phone line. The employee realized that any employee making a complaint was targeted as a disgruntled employee that needed correcting. The assistant manager was promoted to management. Does that mean that Corporate admires and rewards abusive managers? It would make one think so. Do you see the parallel here to old time pre Civil War slavery? The masters choose to perceive not to investigate. The Corporate Ivory Tower is above the plebian ignorant work force. If one does not perceive a problem, there is none.

The lesson learned is that corporations freely hand out fuzzy, feeling good, and wonderful rhetorical buzz words, but rarely abide by them. Verbal abuse and degradation by management is a daily fact and reality of employees that work the front lines. Corporations do not enforce guidelines, values, dignity, and respect to all employees. Even the mid management suffers the slings and arrows from humiliation and disrespect from upper managers. As the old saying goes, "Shit flows downhill."

Nothing can be done to stop abuse until a corporation sets up firm guidelines and accountability for all employees. These guidelines should be established based on issues and not incidents. The guidelines shouldn't be to punish anyone, but provide a positive basis for positive behavioral programs. An employee shouldn't have to worry about being fired or targeted for incidents. Accountability based on understanding that for every action there is a reaction should be the base. Example: If a manager yells at an employee in front of customers, the action, what is the possible reaction? Questions should be asked by management and employees, 'What did the shouting accomplish?' 'Was there a better way to explain the issue?' 'How will this affect the behavior or work of the employees?' 'Did the shouting provide for a more efficient work process?' 'Did this shouting affect other people in listening range like other employees or customers?' 'What do employees think of my behavior?' Insert incident for shouting in any situation. Good management would have these action/reaction guidelines in place for management and employees to use and understand without fear of reprisal. Such protections should be used by corporations for all employees. A set procedure and guidelines should be used for accountability instead of the current verbal and written disciplinary actions.

Disciplinary Action is also a disturbing corporate abuse. Discipline? Really? Employees are adults. Do we need to discipline adults in a work environment? Is discipline for adults in a work environment another form of abusive economic slavery?

Disciplinary action has the connotation of adult workers being childlike and incapable of functioning. The connotation indicates we are not adults. Disciplinary action is another form of degradation. Yet, more and more managers with a need for power and control degrade us with verbal abuse, brow beating, bullying, and these written disciplinary actions to humiliate us into subservience to their wills.

Admittedly this writer is positive action person. There have been times as a manager I had to deal with a good employee that began to bend the rules to a point that required action. This was a good employee. As a manager this person could be replaced, but with her training and current knowledge it would be a loss. Instead, after careful thinking the employee was given two options after an explanation of an issue of lost work time and how that affected the company and peers. The employee took the option to change behavior. Not once was termination mentioned, but in a positive note the employee was told if she chose to focus only on her personal responsibility issue, it would be understood. The employee was told the company would hate to lose a valuable employee, but she would receive an excellent report for new employers once her personal issues were resolved. The choice was the employee's. She chose to stay. The negative focus disappeared. There were no angry words, shouts, or accusations. As an adult the issue was discussed, not the person. It was a positive end to a difficult personal issue. Yes, adults can react to positive discussions. Threats and discipline are bad things in a working environment. Unfortunately we still live in the slave mentality of threat and discipline.

Quick question, 'What exactly is the benefit of a written disciplinary action?' There aren't any real benefits or behavioral changes. The corporations truly don't benefit in work ethics or profit with these written disciplinary actions. When one looks at the written disciplinary actions you will find attacks against an employee. The reaction to the written disciplinary action can be either fear of losing your job, which doesn't benefit the corporation, or anger, which doesn't benefit the corporation. Then why is the written disciplinary action so frequently used by management? It is used for control by management. The giver of the action shows power and control over the life and income of the employee. Submission is the required result. How this submission or acquiescence to any corporate perceived power benefits the bottom line corporate profit is beyond what this author understands.

Yet fear is continually used as a controlling tool of retail corporations. The saddest part is that the corporate executives continue to use plausible deniability of this fear control. What they do not hear or see protects their secluded perfect ivory tower existence.

One of the worst Corporate Abuse is that of **"Customer Service"**. The burden of perceived customer service perfection is placed upon the front line employees. The achievement of perfection in customer service is a nirvana to say the least. Perfect customer service is frankly unobtainable.

'The customer is not always right, the customer is a customer.'
This adage is lost in the halls of the ivory tower executives. What ends up happening is that the corporation actually encourages customers to develop very bad habits. These habits are dangerous as well as bad habits that hurt the bottom line of corporate profits more than the executives could understand.

The customer service focus encourages Corporations to be personally liable for every product they sell. Customer Service removes the customer's accountability for the proper maintenance and responsibility of a purchased product. If an item is bought from a store, although manufactured in China, Hong Kong, India, or even the rare United States item, the customer holds the retail store responsible for the product breaking, tearing, malfunctioning, or not performing as expected. Consider a person putting on a dress that is two sizes to small and a seam rips. The customer immediately returns the product to the retail store as defective. Another customer purchases a pair of tennis shoes and wears them for a year every day, but returns them in a year because the sole fell off (it was obvious the shoes were abused and often wet and muddy) and the pair was only a year old. Consider a retail store customer that returns a gas weed eater because it won't start on the first pull. We won't discuss the customer didn't even read the directions and didn't mix 2 cycle engine oil in with gasoline. The customer never operated a gas weed eater and never bothered to read the directions. After the machine was ruined because of the pure gasoline, it was returned as the store's responsibility.

Does anyone else see the bad habits here?

Standing behind your product is dangerous to the extent that there is a joke in the retail associate world called "Free Rental". A landlord is going to rent an out of town property. The landlord needs to cut the grass while he is at the home location. The landlord buys a lawnmower, cuts the grass, and the next day rents the property. The lawnmower is returned the following day because it is in the time frame of receipt return. What is the customer's reason for the return? "I didn't like it?" A woman buys a dress for a wedding one day and return's it the next. It is in the time frame for receipt. It is called "Free Rental". Another bad habit encouraged by the Corporation in the name of Customer Service.

This customer service also encourages bullying by the customer. The customer doesn't have a clue that this employee can and will lose their job by a complaint. The customer only knows that if he or she is in a bad mood they can go to a retail store to rant and rave at an employee thus getting some type of satisfactory relief for letting off steam.

The bullying is also a Customer Abuse method to make the world fit their demands and special needs. The customer expects any retail employee to fulfill their wish or imminent need instantly or the employee "be damned", literally. There are many stories of a customer planning a party and waiting until the last moment to remember they don't have a grill, propane tank, canopy, charcoal briquettes, or mosquito fogger. The customer comes into the retail store frantically searching for a grill rack that has rusted out and is desperately needed in an hour for the cookout. Unfortunately your store no longer carries that grill or parts because the corporate office has signed up a new vendor. The customer is savage to say the least. They bought the grill from your store and now where is a part they need. It is your personal fault. The anger rages out at the employee and guess what? The customer has to purchase a new grill, one they don't even want or like because it is their emergency. The customer goes home, writes a letter to the corporate office raging about this stupid employee that couldn't help them. Does corporate care the customer was at fault? Definitely not! The employee is spoken too, written up, or fired.

Customers know they can take out their own short comings on any retail employee without fear of retribution. The customer does not know or care that an employee may have to suffer for their mistakes in judgment. The Customer righteously sits at home blaming the employee for their problems. Why? The words, 'Customer Service', mean absolute power to abuse employees as encouraged by the corporations. Corporations will never stand behind an abused employee. It is automatically assumed it is the employee's fault without any investigation or understanding. Simply put, the employee failed at proper customer service even though the customer service was completely out of the control of the employee. The customer never has to take responsibility for their lack of foresight or errors. The customer is exonerated. The reality is that the customer has been encouraged and trained by Corporations to exonerate them from all liability, accountability, and responsibility for their lives. Everything falls upon the employee to make customers a perfect little world that everything is the employee's fault. Do you feel like the *'Whipping Boy'* yet? That is what Customer Service has turned into.

This isn't every customer, but thanks to the encouraging training of the habit through Corporate Customer Service demands, it is becoming more frequent.

In fact, there are times the employee is at fault for lack of customer service, but again it is because it is out of the control of the employee. The majority of employees I know do their best to provide excellent customer service by treating customers as they would like to be treated.

The current bonus systems set for corporate executives and management create another abuse. If a manager wants a large bonus there is one controllable factor to bring the current bonus method up. The manager cuts hours. More and more retail employees are expected to cover larger areas or more departments because there is not enough floor coverage. Employees that are not even knowledgeable of products are thrown into the pit to help customers. The customers want answers on a product and are given wrong information or no information because the person covering that department doesn't have a clue how to answer a question on a product. The regular and trained employee in that department has had the hours cut from their schedule. The Corporate Bonus System encourages bad abusive habits for their management. Bonus is determined by bottom line profit numbers. A bonus is never determined by innovation, creative marketing, accessing store environment and personnel attributes.

Here is an example of lack of store coverage. An angry customer came into the department furious that his grass had completely died. The trained department employee quickly learned that the customer was offered four products for their lawn and was not informed about the dangers of putting on three separate products at the same time during the hottest part of the day. A trained employee would have first understood the main problem, which in this case was a lawn disease, offered the correct solution and warned the customer to only use the fungicide in late afternoon before sunset and not when it was raining or about to rain. Instead because of bad advice, the man put fertilizer, herbicide, insecticide, and fungicide on his lawn at the same time and watered them all down in mid afternoon. The employee never remarked at the wrong advice, but focused only on the immediate problem to bring his lawn back to life with correct information. Suggestions were made and discussed. A month later the customer came back to thank the employee because his lawn had returned and looked healthy and green.

Don't think the customer contacted the corporate office about the success, the customer may not have even written about the disaster, but it was in this case lack of proper customer service due to the corporate cutbacks for higher managerial bonus. Do you believe corporations will ever bite the bullet and accept responsibility for bad bonus decisions resulting in poor customer service? Don't hold your breath.

Instead the corporations have developed a new buzz word called *cross training*. Retail floor associates are expected to be crossed trained to be back up cashiers and cashiers are expected to be cross trained as floor employees. Did anyone hear a man cannot serve two masters? Is it really possible to cross train employees to the extent they are superior in many positions and know everything in many positions? Does the employee even have an interest in cross training? Yes some do, but some don't. What the corporations really end up with are laissez faire employees. The managers have big bonus money, but the employees are abused and deal with stress while customer service falters. The employees may get bonus from some retail corporations, but the bonus is small compared to the management and corporate bonus.

Another negative practice of major corporations is percentage bonus and raise monies. Every worker gets an across the board percent raise. It doesn't matter if one employee works at customer service or works hard at their job. An employee receives the same percentage raise that the chronically late, complaining, and or incompetent worker receives. Why bother to excel? The percentages are made in the fiscal planning sessions and have absolutely nothing to do with individual work ethics or reviews.

The continual changing of managers is not only abuse, it creates havoc. The chaos of management change is actually inhibitive to the bottom line. It is beyond comprehension that corporations have lost all sense of loyalty and appreciation for knowledge. The focus on number crunching and bean counting is detrimental to corporations, but they cannot see it. Managers used to manage. In the Corporate Abusive mind set today, the word manage means balance the bottom line with profit.

Constant managerial changing does not enhance the work floor. It creates new baggage, new agendas, and floor disruption. The associates knew what was expected and what to do upon entering the floor. Suddenly a new manager enters with new agendas and rules tells the associates what they have done prior is now wrong.

The corporation believes without change things get stagnant. This is true, but constant disruption and management style change is just more disruptive, if not more than stagnation.

Personality is very much a part of an employee whether it is in corporate, mid management, or front line worker. A worker will get used to a personality good or bad. When the personality is changed suddenly there is too much time wasted adjusted to the new personality, style, and agenda.

There is a better way for corporate to change management. That way is slowly integrate new management. Have the new management work side by side with the old manager and learn the personality of the store, its market, its customers, and its workers. Wouldn't it be better if the manager interacted not only with the assistant managers and supervisors, but the front line employee asking about the typical customer of the store and phases of sales or products? Isn't that a better way? Instead, the corporations slice the personality of the store with a dull razor. One size does not fit all.

Corporate Agendas

I could never understand exactly what the management agenda is for any retail corporate store I have ever worked.

The dictionary defines agenda as: *–noun, formally a plural of* agendum, *but usually used as a singular with plural* -das *or* -da.
a list, plan, outline, or the like, of things to be done, matters to be acted or voted upon, etc.

Employees receive lists of work to be done, matters to acted upon, and work schedules. To me the lists of work to be done are verbal, handwritten, or computer printouts are edicts. There is never a discussion with employees. Management shares no plans or visions. Many times the corporate super buys are processed down the line to the old adage of the floor associates stuffing 10 lbs of shit in a 5 lb bag. The employee is allowed no interaction with management as to planning or creativity. The corporate world will allow suggestion boxes, but very little creativity with employees and management occurs. Yet, the new "Y" generation is lauded for creativity and hard work that dictates to corporations their time and pay. I've yet to see hard work and creativity in low wage positions. The "Y" generation does indeed dictate to corporations their time and pay.

This does not mean employees do not practice creative thought and idea action. An employee is many times required to place objects in one place to another without pre planned space allotment. The creativity by the employee is usually genius. Displays by employees are creative. The employee rarely gets recognition for such creativity. It should be noted here that many times creativity is not acceptable behavior by management. Any deviation from their preconceived ideas about a corporate plan is strictly forbidden.

My perception of Retail Corporate Management is that of only one focus, gluttony. Management focuses on the bonus. The current bonus structure of retail corporations is based on manipulations of a juggling act of employee hours and store projections. Employee hours are the only controlling variable in a management tool kit because bonus is based on numbers, not creativity or knowledge management. Therefore, employees must suffer to bring in larger bonus to the corporation and management.

There is never a thought of efficiency. The happier and content the employee, a greater loyalty and efficiency will be provided to the employer. That simple knowledge and understanding has been completely lost in the oligarchy world of the 21st Century Corporate World. The employee as a tool to be treated with reverence and care is gone the way of the dinosaur. Today's corporate world is that of economic slavery.

My favorite song is Tennessee Ernie Fords "16 Tons". "St. Peter don't you call me cause I can't go. I owe my soul to the company store". We will work until we die, just as the slaves did in the early years of America.

The Corporate offices only see the world in a one size fits all vision. The corporation makes no allowances for store location, square footage, bay design, and floor design. The product market area and population social economic level also influence a store's personality. The design of all retail corporate stores is unique. Two women can wear a size 12, but are shaped completely differently. One is tall and weighs 180 lbs. The other is short and weighs 125 lbs. The dress length is not going to fit the tall size 12 or the short size 12. Why is this concept so difficult for corporations to understand? A store located in South Florida is not going to sell insulated underwear and heavy coats year round any more than a store located in New York is going to sell bikinis year round. Selling tractors in a tight city area is not going to work as well as selling tractors in a more rural suburb, but the same tractors are found in each store. Why should a store have a snow blower for sale in Southern Texas? In Wisconsin, Minnesota, Upper New York, and the New England States, the snow blower is a must have.

The same is true with corporate attitudes about their employees. The corporate see the worker as a one size fits all. Weather makes a difference and so does area sub culture. People in Wisconsin are generally somber and suspicious much like Maine people. California people are more laid back. New York people are hyper in action and conversations. Yes, these are generalities, but that is my point. One size does not fit all.

The corporate rules are a one size fits all.

"SEX, SEX, AND MORE SEX WITH AN ADDITION OF AGE AND SEX DISCRIMINATION"

Running rampant in retail store management are sexual predators. It isn't anything new or different and nothing has changed. That is the truly sad part.

One has to admit that globally this is a man's world. To this day men receive more pay, chances for advancement, and a power respect given by this society. We are trained from childhood on with an attitude that men are smarter, more capable. We give the male specie power by rite, not by capability.

One must keep in mind though; the wages of the American workforce is decreasing since the 1970's. There is a slight elevation of salary, but research has proven that to be increased working hours. The majority of increased working hours are the addition of women normally remaining at home in the occupational career of wife and mother integrating into the workforce.

This is not to say the balance should be given to females. Balance should be achieved by knowledge and capability of position. It is also a fact that because of completely different upbringings of the sexes, women score higher in certain managerial levels than men. Men may score higher in other levels than women. Physically women are built differently than men. Therefore men are more adept in certain physical pursuits than women. Conversely, in higher level thinking women could have more adept skills. The problem is that positions and attitudes are not rated on capability or skill. Continually the corporations slant higher salaries and positions to male sexual bias.

To the disgrace of our supposed advanced society, corporations do not run at high levels of efficiency because of this sexual prejudice. This also gives the male management a sexual predatory power that should not be allowed or given. The corporations do not realize the abuse of this predation, nor do they stop it. Instead the corporations perpetuate the abuse.

For several years I have been observing the sexual interactions of male managers and female employees. The results are predictable. A sexual affair is initiated and ended. Fortunately it is rare that a child is created with such affairs, but it does happen. The affair is rarely, but occasionally brought to an undeniable attention of upper management or executive management. The management then slaps the hands of the male, since "Boys will be Boys" and the female is terminated from her position, because the behavior of the female is considered to be "unladylike". The male manager is then transferred to another location.

I have never comprehended this attitude since it is a "lose-lose" situation for the corporation. The fact the corporation does not understand this is mind boggling. I openly admit I do not have a master's degree in business, but quite logically the transferred male manager does not provide the corporation a true benefit if the manager is obviously predatory.

One example is a retail corporation manager known to me. This manager was transferred to another store after a disastrous affair with a female supervisor. The executive management fired the woman and put this male manager in a new store. It was immediately obvious to most employees in the store that this male manager was again on the hunt for a young attractive female. Apparently this male manager had several in his rifle scope. One of the hunted was married. The others were not.

What benefit does a male manager provide to the full operating function of the corporation when the manager is spending most of his time hunting females? Moving the manager to another store only gives the predator a fresh hunting ground. I am reminded of the condemnation of the Catholic Church and how they fall under constant criticism for the same practice. The predatory priests are only moved to a different church. How does that solve the problem? The corporations are not any different.
23

This is not to put full blame on the male manager. An intelligent woman would be aware of these advances and ignore them. A woman would not allow her reputation or position to be endangered by such predation. Unfortunately there are the starlets who share the casting couch with hope of advancement. A male manager does have power with advancing and wage increases. A producer and director can propel a starlet skyward. We all know this.

The male is wrong to use power and advance to get sexual favors. The woman is also wrong to use her body to achieve power and advance. However, this will never end until the Corporations clearly write down rules and guidelines to protect the male and female from predation. Unfortunately the corporations will never do such a thing until they realize such behaviors actually inhibit their bottom line and efficiency. To this day there are only vague rules and guidelines regarding sexual harassment and sexual abuse. The medieval rule of men are chastised and women are punished continues today.

It is difficult for me to stand righteously condemning Islam religion for abuse of women when in so many ways Christian faith is just as cruel. The Christian corporate executives' self- righteously claims benevolence when in fact there is blatant sexual predation and discrimination that goes on every day in the retail business.

I have heard stories of female workers walking in on male managers having sex with female employees in back rooms, cars, nearby locations. Even some male workers have told me of flagrant sexual abuse by management they have witnessed. The married male workers were disgusted.

There is no turning in of such information, because the environment is set up to disavow the information. It is impossible to bring facts to the attention of the corporation, because there are no guidelines as to presentation of the facts. Everything in such cases is your word against mine and who will they believe? Will corporates believe an employee or a manager? The proof of evidence is too difficult to achieve for employees to present to corporations. But the beat goes on. The working environment becomes difficult for other workers.

Why does the environment turn hostile for other employees? It is simple. During the affair the female associate does receive special treatment from the male manager. The female often flaunts the special treatment and supposed power. Other employees become afraid of the employee, and rightly so. If there is any disagreement or assigned task the affair employee objects too, a simple complaint to the male manager takes care of it. The other employees have to walk on tiptoes around the special treatment employee. Ergo, work is not productive or beneficial to the corporation.

It is truly a phenomenon to observe when certain male management hires new employees. Certain male managers prefer young black women and the majority of new hires are young black women. Then the gossip begins when a young attractive black woman begins an affair with a middle aged manager. Another prefers young Spanish women, and then there is an increase in those hires. The manager is transferred or advanced and the next thing you know, a different male manager starts hiring young white women. It is obvious to the workers these affairs go on, but apparently the executive management itself remains blind-sided.

I am consistently reminded that this is the way of the world. The entire world is patriarchal and nothing will change. Women not only are continually abused and misused; most of the women perpetuate the power of a patriarchal society.

The patriarchal society is also an immense inhibitor to the capability of an older woman. Older men continue to be prized in the retail industry more than older women. The slanted reasoning is that older men have more knowledge and experience. The women are looked upon as less valuable without any credit for knowledge or experience. The most valuable employee in current retail businesses is the young strong male. Just as in the years of American slavery, a higher value was put on a muscular young male slave. In second place is a young pretty female, so it is better pickings not only for the male supervisors and managers, but male customers in the bargain. The older male employees are looked upon with reverence as experienced. The older female is looked upon as incapable and insignificant with a hope to simply get rid of them either by continual harassment of write ups for the least infraction (perception) or the employee getting so fed up with the harassment, she quits.

Yes, older female employees are harassed. An older female employee receives write ups for any little thing such as mere comment, while younger attractive females can actually blatantly be disrespectful without a raised eyebrow. An older female employee will be written up for being five minutes late or an hour late, while the younger female employees virtually come in on their own schedules and call out if they lost their lipstick that day (Okay, that is a bit of an exaggeration.)

A younger female co-worker snapped angrily back at a supervisor after he requested her to give him her phone. In front of customers, she angrily replied, "I don't need an attitude from you." An eyebrow wasn't even raised. Another co-worker, older female on the heavy side, but not obese, tripped on a hose and hurt her arm. She was written up for not following safety rules? What? Yet another younger female, currently rumored to be having an affair with a male manager, was given four months light duty after twisting an ankle. Nobody said the world was fair, but age, weight, and sex prejudices are high in the retail corporate world and there is absolutely nothing one can do about it.

Even the customers are extremely prejudicial. If a female employee is standing next to any male, `old or young, the customer directs their question at the male. It is as if the female employee does not exist or simply are too stupid to help them. The female customer is the worse. Generally, one out of hundred male customers does not care if the employee is female and directs the question to the employee. A female customer one hundred out of one hundred will direct the question to a male before a female. I have pondered the reason for this and came to the conclusion that we are all raised in the same patriarchal society but in America it is worse simply because of jealousy. It is difficult for most women to engage in sisterhood as do other women of the world. Most of the American females are jealous of the fact another female might know more than they do. That is really a sad thought, since all of all us learn new things every day and it is a good thing to share knowledge.

A very subtle and cruel corporate abuse is discussed above in the management abuse, but the Corporation precipitates the environment. The constant rotation of managers around stores can be extremely abusive to the associates. Every manager has his or ((rarely) her agendas). The managers create havoc with their moves and own agendas. These management agendas have little or nothing to do with corporate agendas or objectives.

These management agendas are personal and parallel their secret desires, wishes, sadism, or ego. All of the above.

The top requirement of store managers is not loyalty, knowledge, or management skills. The top requirement of store managers from corporate is number crunching and goal achievements. To these ends the store managers pursue the goals and numbering crunching with not only relish, but zealotry. Just like most zealots, the blood spilled before them in achievement of these goals is unimportant.

The current corporate manager only sees numbers, not people, not lives, not families, not humanity. To current store managers we are nothing more than numbers. To the corporation we are nothing more than numbers. We the numbers are to be bent, broken, bruised, humiliated, cajoled, lied to, abused, walked upon, and enslaved for the greater good of the corporation. The overseers will do everything cruel and necessary to achieve the Massah's goals. Just like the Civil War slaves, we the economic slaves are not viewed as people. We are as President George Herbert Walker Bush called us, "Fodder." We are the economic "Fodder" slaves of the corporation.

Respect is One Way in a Corporate Street

The corporate retail world has respect as a core value. This value is respect for the Manager. When it comes to respect for an individual, all is lost. This word requires its own chapter since the word is bandied about so much in the corporate retail world. What is the actual meaning of respect and which definition do you refer when discussing RESPECT as a core value. Below are the meanings of Respect from Dictionary.com.

re·spect

Show Spelled[ri-**spekt**] ?Show IPA

noun

1.

a particular, detail, or point (usually preceded by *in*): *to differ in some respect.*

2.

relation or reference: *inquiries with respect to a route.*

3.

esteem for or a sense of the worth or excellence of a person, a personal quality or ability, or something considered as a manifestation of a personal quality or ability: *I have great respect for her judgment.*

4.

deference to a right, privilege, privileged position, or someone or something considered to have certain rights or privileges; proper acceptance or courtesy; acknowledgment: *respect for a suspect's right to counsel; to show respect for the flag; respect for the elderly.*

5.

the condition of being esteemed or honored: *to be held in respect.*

EXPAND

6.

respects, a formal **expression** or gesture of greeting, esteem, or friendship: *Give my respects to your parents.*

7.

favor or partiality.

8.

Archaic . a consideration.

COLLAPSE

---

verb (used with object)
9.
to hold in esteem or honor: *I cannot respect a cheat.*
10.
to show regard or consideration for: *to respect someone's rights.*
11.
to refrain from intruding upon or interfering with: *to respect a person's privacy.*
12.
to relate or have reference to.

It would appear that corporations use definition four for the core value. The management believes deference is a right of their privileged position. Respect has no other meaning in the corporate world. I have always believed that respect is both. There is respect for who have earned the privilege and for one self in holding values to your honor and self esteem.

Time and time again the respect issue is only about managerial position, just for the position and not for the actions of the management or manager. The slave had to show deference to the master simply because of the master's position of wealth and power. So it is with retail corporations. Respect is deference to the manager or supervisor simply because of the position of power. It certainly would be advantageous of corporations to explain that value in those terms instead of letting us believe that respect is consideration, esteem, deference, quality, or ability of all workers.

Foolishly I believed, and certainly many others believed that Respect was a two way street. I have since learned most disastrously that respect is only about management simply because of their position and not their actions. Throughout this book it becomes quite clear how we in the 21st Century are economically enslaved and how parallel our lives are controlled in similarity to the slavery of the Civil War Era.

Wouldn't it have been quite easy to write in employee handbooks that respect is given to management just because they have the position of management? An employee has to respect the position even if the management abuses that privilege.

I had no idea that it was perfectly acceptable to allow managers to yell in anger at workers in front of customers. I had no idea that it was acceptable for managers to demean, browbeat, intimidate, and bully workers still demanding respect for a position. It is however a fact. I have always felt that we earned respect by treating each other with consideration of values. How very wrong could one person be?

Understanding my misunderstanding of the Respect definition I realize that retail managers have the privilege of respect simply because of the position. It is wrong of me to question an authority to intimidate, bully, and threaten a worker. If only the corporation would define the Respect value more specifically we poor lowly enslaved workers should know better than even look at a Massah much less hope he respects us for our duty, loyalty, and work.

Harassment, Diversity, and Disparity

For any corporation to say they are equal opportunity is a corporate illusion. With the onset of online employment application computers may give the façade of impartiality, but there is still the human factor behind the keyboard.

After the computer analyzes the applicant's information and responses, the computer prints out the analysis. Humans take the print outs and determinations are made for area hires. From the area districts, the printouts are divided in location and then to store management. What happens between the computer printout and the individual store hiring manager can be any number of things. Will more Hispanic applicants be chosen in a certain area because in this location the stores have primarily Hispanic populations? Are Black applicants sent to other locations for certain stores for their primary customers? Are certain ages chosen at a certain time to fill obligatory requirements from the United States Government? Are any of these applications profiled for such purpose? Only the Corporate Headquarters could answer this, but I am certain there would be little fact and a great deal of rhetoric.

Primarily though, the disparity begins with the actual retail store. The choice of hiring is dependent upon the prejudices of the hiring manager and the manager of the store. Even if the manager is a certain area of a significant racial profiling, the manager still selects employees based on personal hiring prejudice.

Looking in the past of eight managers in eight years at one particular store, the hiring has been slanted to the specific prejudice of the manager and the hiring manager. In the first manager, married to a Hispanic woman, there was a majority of Hispanic associates. Then it was followed by another manager for Black associates. Several managers then preferred Caucasian associates, now we are back to Hispanic associates once more. And once more the associates are pressured to learn Spanish for the Hispanic clientele, the manager is Hispanic. Of course management selects the edict from corporate headquarters that the Spanish population purchases more per visit than other races. It is corporate that wants the Hispanic population elevated and one must learn their language.

There are articles written that expound upon the facts that the Hispanic population spends more per capita of their income than any other racial group. Therefore the corporations focus on the Hispanic market. Of course the corporations forget the other varied markets or racial ethnicity comprise a greater sum of expenditures even though they do not spend the same percentage of their income as the Hispanics. Can we believe what these marketing experts expound about the Hispanics? The corporations seem to believe considering the pressure to change the spoken and written language of American English to a country of a country to Spanish. These experts divide the ethnicity into specific groups of Caucasian, African American, Native American, Asian, and Hispanic.

Combine the lower percentage of three groups, with the higher percentage of one group and you are ignoring the higher actual dollar of the other three. Is there ever any logic to the analysis by these supposed marketing experts?

Throughout major corporations in American there is a new agenda. It is Racial Profiling. Of course this is good racial profiling, right? I say wrong. Racial Profiling is wrong no matter what purpose is put upon it. Corporations are now requesting that employees learn to communicate in Spanish for the Hispanic market. The Corporations say they want to serve the needs our special Hispanic customers. Surveys have shown that Hispanic people spend 44% more than other racial counterparts. Really? Did anyone ever say, "Analyze this?" Consider the fact that Hispanic lumps Puerto Ricans, Cubans, Mexicans, Brazilians, Spanish, Portuguese, Chileans, Costa Ricans, Panamanians, Ecuadorians, Argentineans, etc. together. Has anyone looked that closely at Irish, English, Scots, Welsh, Belize, French, Russian, German, Polish, Norwegians, Swedish, Netherlanders, Greenlanders, Canadians, Belize, and other etc. Caucasians lumped together? Have these statistics lumped Asians like Japanese, Chinese, Islanders, Pilipino, Indonesians, Cambodians, Vietnamese, Fiji, New Zealanders, Aborigines, Native Americans, Mid Easterners, East Indians, etc? May be if all these racial diversities were clumped together that 44% more wouldn't be.

When Arizona wanted to go after illegal immigrants, it was called racial profiling the Mexicans. Yes that is wrong. If you want to go after illegal immigrants, there are scores of illegal Russians, East Indians, Vietnamese, Chinese, etc. An illegal immigrant is precisely that, an illegal immigrant. Then why is it acceptable and supported with pressure to racially profile a shopping group. A shopper is a shopper after all. Pushing workers to learn a foreign language, considering the official language of the United States is English, because of racial profiling is just plain wrong. Racial Profiling is Racial Profiling and regardless the course, it is just wrong.

The end result is pressure on the people that work the frontlines at the exact point of purchase. While pressured to focus on one group, the other groups are aggravated and irritated. There are many times customers have grumbled about the Spanish broadcast on the speakers. Surprisingly it is the Asian cultural group that is the most irritated. The complaint is the same, "I couldn't come to this country until I learned to speak, read, and write English. It is disgusting."

The pressure to learn Spanish has become nearly harassment. The associate is forced to take web lessons and carry translation booklets to greet all customers in Spanish. Already the majority of new associates in our particular location store are Hispanic. They speak in Spanish to each other in the break room, on the sales floor, and on the radio. The English speaking associates are completely left in the dark regarding the conversation. This is not the best way to communicate with everyone to accomplish tasks. The English speaking associate is put at a disadvantage to assist customers and doing required tasks. The result is the Hispanic and English speaking associate has advantage over the English speaking associate. The accolades continually slant to the Hispanic associate workforce. Is this on purpose?

We do not live in Mexico or Panama. We live in America, and the American worker is being harassed. Is it good to be bilingual? Yes it is, but to be forced into learning a different language is simply wrong. If it is necessary to learn another language and be bilingual, the workforce should be allowed to choose the language. Many Asians have a second language of French. Should we learn to speak French? What about Canadian stores? Must Canadians speak both English and French?

Depending upon the location one lives determines the pressure applied to learn Spanish for the customers. That is disparity. The Pressure is Harassment. All of this because some marketing expert determined that one ethnicity spends a higher percentage than four others. Did these marketing experts look at clumps ethnicity, or just individualize the ethnics when comparing buying statistics with the clumped Hispanic ethnic group?

Currently in Corporate America there is a new harassment of the elder worker. In some corporate expert's mind, the elder and the obese worker must go. The reasons are economic, the corporations explain. The elder and obese are higher health risks and the premiums cost more. These elder employees have also been longer in the work force and have higher wages.

This is just plain nonsense. The younger generation begins work at nearly the same wages it took many of the elder employees those long years of service to obtain. An example would be that ten years ago an employee started at wage of $7.25 per hour. Today that elder employee earns $9.75 per hour. The new employee comes in at $9.25 to $9.50 per hour. The company is only .25 ahead.

The elder employee has health issues, but so does the young family. Those babies that keep being born under the insurance cost just as much and generally more, since the new mothers take the new baby in at least two to four times a month for standard care and every time the child has an earache, sniffle, cough, or temperature. Today's infant generation sees a doctor and has more ailments than ever before. Cancer does not strike only the elder, the ratio is equal for children. The elder do have maintenance medicines, but those are generally cheaper than the new fancy pharmaceuticals for the children.

The push is on to rid the workplace of the elder. The most highly targeted group is the elder woman. If the elder woman is overweight it is even worse. The harassment of the management is nightmarish. There isn't even an infraction of any rules, but there are perception and personal written disciplinary actions.

Here are a few of the disparity between the young and the elder associate. A young associate sets their own hours. The young associate shows up at any unscheduled time, works the time they chose for the day, and nothing happens. The new workforce is used to their time, not the scheduled time. It is the new youth work ethic. The elder obese woman is written up simply because once in eight years she wrote down the wrong time for the schedule and was an hour late.

The clothes acceptable for the younger associate are not at all in the dress code. Clearly extreme hairdo, cut hole jeans, fancy shoes, pants down below the hip line, underwear showing, T-shirts, no collars, see thru lace blouses, caps of all sorts. The elder obese woman must adhere strictly to the dress code or receives a written disciplinary action.

A younger associate can argue, be sarcastic, and completely ignore tasks without reprisal. The elder obese female is under attack consistently. The elder obese female is targeted to the point of regardless the answer to any managerial or supervisorial question is written up as a disciplinary action for being unprofessional and disrespectful to the manager or supervisor.

As an example, an elder obese associate was sitting on a stool while performing the duty of greeter station. Some stores allow associates to sit while greeting, others do not. There is no corporate dictate regarding that matter, but in this case this store did not allow greeters to sit unless the younger female was pregnant(note: the young female was pregnant – special treatment in today's corporation, not back thirty or forty years ago.) The stool had been left there, since one of the greeters had been pregnant. The elder obese woman sat on the stool and was asked in front of customers why she was sitting by an assistant manager. She told the manager the truth. The woman was tired, elder, and not feeling well. Within an hour the elder obese woman was called in to the manager's office and received a written disciplinary action for disrespect to a manager. The next day, the employee had succumbed to the excessive heat and humidity. The employee collapsed in the store and was caught from falling onto the concrete floor by a customer. The elder obese woman received a written excuse from the doctor to stay out of the heat and humidity. The employee then could sit when greeting. The male manager was furious, but the disciplinary action remained.

Another ugly management abuse that rears its ugly head is discrimination and disparity. The subtly discriminatory practices are so individual to store and management they are extremely evasive. To catch the discrimination or disparity is as difficult as an oiled man trying to catch a greased pig.

There are a number of Caribbean workers in the U.S. that work on Island time. In other words they come in at their convenience ignoring their schedules. That is the island way. It works in Caribbean stores. It does not work in metropolitan stores. Yet, the Caribbean worker is never counseled or written up for maintaining the island way in a metropolitan store. A metropolitan worker in a metropolitan store is written up for coming in seven minutes late. The islander behavior is acceptable to management, where the metropolitan worker coming in just a few minutes late is not.

Each store manager, assistant manager, middle manager, supervisor, etc. brings along discriminatory baggage. Since these managers jump from store to store or even promoted to higher levels, the discrimination is hardly noticed. It is only the discriminated employees that feel the discrimination. Race is a discrimination bias that is shown when a certain racial manager takes over. One manager is Hispanic and dislikes Blacks and Europeans. Another is White and dislikes Hispanics and Mexicans. Another is Black and dislikes Whites and Orientals. Some young managers have hard prejudices against older employees. Other managers don't like heavy or obese employees. The treatment of such discriminated employees is extremely evident in retail stores. These employees must live in hostile environments, worry about getting written actions for even the most minor infractions, never receive equal raises, and literally in some cases, bullied by the discriminating manager. There are managers that will write up a disciplinary action for an employee wearing a ball cap backwards, while other employees can wear different sorts of unattractive headwear. Ripped jeans, t-shirts, and underwear revealing low pants, are acceptable. Yet, a well endowed older woman is reprimanded and written up for showing too much cleavage.

The management baggage encourages harassment as individual as their baggage with no recourse for the employee being harassed. Instead, the employee hangs on by a thread if not fired, and waits until the new management comes along with new baggage. The employee hopes the new manager can harass a different group for awhile.

The saddest part of this harassment and discrimination baggage is that the burden of proof is on the employees. Every employee is so afraid of losing their job that they just endure and will not support each other to unite against the harassment. There is no Human Resource for the employee. In Corporate America today there is the "open door policy" otherwise known as a Faux Pas. If you use the open door, you are the FOE (Faux). There is no protection for the employee. The discrimination is unique to the current manager and there is no way to stop them or write them up for the abuse or discrimination.

It is very strange that while employees are evaluated once, twice, or several times a year, that there is no counter evaluation of management. Yes, they are evaluated, but not the same way as front line employees. I have heard of managers writing their own evaluations, or the managers having other managers write a manager's evaluation. We wish front line employees could do that. We know who works, who doesn't, and who is privileged. If we could all write honest evaluations or make each other top notch by writing our own, it would be really wonderful.

The employee surveys given on occasion are a joke. The Surveys are set up questions that make management look good. The survey company gives a corporation a win-win package.

There should be a management evaluation set up for employees. The evaluations should be made on measurable and day to day operations of the retail store. How about questions like, is your manager often visible on the floor? *Yes No Occasionally.* Does your manager know the department? *Yes No Learning.* Does your manager project a civil demeanor with you? With customers? Can you count on your manager to assist with stock issues? Customer issues? Operation issues? Are tasks assigned in priority basis? Does your manager have good time management skills? Are you comfortable discussing store issues with your manager? Does your manager set aside time for discussion when needed? Where can your manager improve in store knowledge, time management, employee relations, customer service, etc. Questions I would love to see and answer would be. In a few words describe your store manager- *A Baptist minister preaching the Gospel.* Describe your department assistant manager- *Flighty* Describe your supervisor *–Lazy with a huge superiority complex* Describe your OPS manager- *Self involved and leaning toward discriminatory prejudices.* Describe your Special Orders manager *– Egotistical, depraved, predatory, megalomaniacal, sadistic, bully, and has major psychological issues.*

Is Customer Service the sole responsibility of the floor employee, or shouldn't management and corporate management take some accountability. *Mommy says no, so ask Daddy and Daddy says yes? It happens a lot with customers and the front line associate looks like the bad evil person to the customer.*

We are aware that store managers ride the flesh of assistant managers, who ride the backs of supervisors, and all of the above ride the backs of floor employees. Everyone has their own agenda and baggage that really have nothing to do with operations of a store or customer service. Somewhere there should be regulation because currently floor employees as well as managers and supervisors are subject to "Sand Lot Baseball rules". The rules change with the change. The pressure and hostile environment is horrendous.

The corporation continues to maintain a blind eye to the abuses of rules as long as the number crunching continues to provide profit.

The Last Chapter

Hostile Environment and the

Intimidation of Bullying Managers.

It is at this moment I have determined that I can no longer work for the retail store I was employed. The Environment has become so hostile it is truly unbearable. I thought if I brought down my availability to few hours it would ease contact with bullying managers. It has always been an issue with me to obstinacy regarding unfair treatment of employees. I had also wanted to keep my vision insurance which is actually good coverage. Unfortunately I can no longer serve the company or its customers under such incredible bullying, intimidation, and race-age-sexual bias. Let it be known that I turned in my resignation under duress.

Again, I repeat this is my perception and how I see it. I must ask though, is this factual? The evidence of fact seems to hold firm. The other question in my mind is the corporate office aware of this, encourage it, promote it, or dictate it? Is it the corporate, district, or regional offices policy? In the store I worked, it is definitely a policy and practice.

I have been writing this book for several years and because of my recent decision to resign, it was time to finish, release, and share my perceptions with others in the public.

Going into the history of a store I would explain that there have been eight managers in nine years in this particular store. Explained prior is the upheaval such change in command causes. Each manager comes in with their own agenda, bias, and rules. Each manager has their own priority for advancement monetarily and promotion. I have noticed in these nine years that any manager worthy of the title of manager or assistant manager is quickly discharged or leaves the company for a different corporation. It does make me wonder if the corporate office does indeed prefer bullying and intimidation methods for worker control. It is a known practice to use fear as a controller of workers. Particularly in this current economic time of high unemployment using fear of losing one's job is an excellent intimidation.

What the corporations do not understand is that some of the management they give this power actually delight in the power and control over those they conceive to be weak. It is to them a real high to bully and intimidate workers. These people derive pleasure from the power given and use it on every occasion they can. It is a drug to them. Previously stated, there is no recourse for any employee to seek relief. The open powers corporations give their management bullies to thrive in is vast. It is only when the management is actually caught in an act such as personal – sexual involvement with a subservient employee is action taken. Usually it is only after undeniable documentation with a child produced or photographic evidence does the corporations actually respond to the issue. The result is generally the male is moved to another location, (fresh pickings), and the female is discharged. It is only after undeniable documentation does the corporation respond. That is not the case with workers. Mere hearsay or personal bias and prejudice by a customer or manager are enough to discharge any worker. What a manager perceives is the law. It is not different than the dark ages when a lord was in a bad mood and decided he didn't like a certain servant, slave, or serf. The worker was tortured, maimed, or killed on the whim of the lord. I might add that verbal abuse is torture.

Because of these managerial actions of bias and entanglements, the hostile environments exist for the rest of the workers. An example would be where a female worker had a fling with an assistant manager. Everyone knew of the affair and to this day, when the female worker is told something by her immediate supervisor that she is not happy with, she calls the assistant manager. The female worker always gets her way after the call. The other workers know not to cross her because she would definitely put them in trouble. That dear reader is a hostile environment and if you work retail you are most certainly aware of it. The corporations do absolutely nothing to prevent such an environment.

Nor do corporations do anything to prevent bias hostile environments from happening. In the store I worked in for almost nine years, I gave my all to be a good employee. I learned the department on my own and learned on my own the answers to many questions my customers had that weren't taught in computer training. To this day the department booklet test I wrote the answers for is the standard guide for all new workers. The computer training teaches product brand, not knowledge. I left my part time position on my work days feeling good that I had helped a customer with knowledge to help them and their issues. I read and learned to become a better tool for the corporation. All this was thrown away by the corporation by allowing "management discretion" in "counseling" that was every bit intimidating, abrasive, and abusive bullying. When you know "counseling" could very well affect your health to the point of dire consequences for you, it is time to leave even though you need the income.

There are other things learned in a retail world. About half of the men and women customers truly believe that only a man can have knowledge about products, unless one works in a chic shop. Some women resent a woman knowing about things that they do not. Part of good salesmanship is sensing the customer and knowing when to back off. Some supervisors resent knowledge and skill of female employees, because it shakes their ego. Sales skills are rarely used or recognized in a large corporate retail world. The focus is primarily on numbers, products, not skills, and not people. There are intelligent and capable men that are supervisors. These men have been passed over continually as "non promotable" for several years. Perhaps the corporation has noted these managers are not capable of intimidation, fear, and bullying? Perhaps these managers truly are good managers and supervisors so the corporations do not want to promote them because of their excellent performance. Currently, recent hires with little knowledge or capability have come in as employees and instantly been promoted to supervisory positions. Two new male Hispanics come to a store from other stores and in two months are promoted to supervisors. (Racial Disparity from a Hispanic Manager? Who could prove it?) I do not know if this is store, district, region, or even corporate has dictated the policy. I do know that with this change I notice stores suffering from out of stocks and return to an unorganized filthy store. The knowledgeable supervisors do their best to keep up the store, but even though a store is showing great profit, it is an illusion to the ultimate collapse of a quality store.

Large corporate retail stores also cannot comprehend the power of loyalty. Large corporate retail stores no longer understand the value of tools (their workers). Loyalty and tool value is only found with the appreciation of the tool. The appreciation is not in just words, but in proper care. More and more corporations are taking away benefits that would inspire good employees to seek them as employers. Less benefits, lower pay, and removal of holiday and vacation days are part of the lack of care by corporations to employees. It is all about the gluttonous profit, and nothing to do with the value of their tools. "You get what you pay for." The corporations that deny proper care to their tools will soon learn those tools will not function properly and the end result will be the lack of the ability of corporations to exist. Continual bias of stores regarding specific races, ages, and sex is another crisis about to happen. Without a proper mix and quality care of all tools, will be a result in the lack of the ability of a corporation to function.

A retail corporation decided to support an Islam TV reality show. The backlash from Christian fundamentalists was so intense, the store backed away from sponsorship. I guess it is bad to sponsor Islam, but good to sponsor the Hispanics? I have heard the corporation backed out because the reality show was bad. Isn't that a matter of taste? I admit that I don't watch any reality show and think they are all bad and in poor taste. TV has Chinese, East Indian, Islam, and Hispanic stations to name a few. This diversity is out of hand. Where does it end? Doesn't diversity mean to divide? I could hardly go to France and expect everything to be in American English, now could I? What if I went to Spain and demanded everything and every store speak American English?

One bias of which is spoken of above is that of a specific target, white older women with weight and or health issues. There is extreme bias just on weight issues alone. The assumption is made that anyone with a weight issue is stupid and slovenly, for women this is even a higher rating in prejudice. The following are only the instances I am personally and currently aware of. I was acquainted with one very intelligent woman working only on weekends. She spoke five languages and had great experience in cashiering. She was Caucasian, older, and heavy set. She was harassed constantly every weekend and written up for some lame accusation every weekend for months. Finally she had enough and quit. Another older female, Caucasian, and heavy set, female was fired after being targeted with supposed customer complaints was discharged. She had been with the company for a long time. Recently another elder, Caucasian, not too heavy set, female, but with health issues was discharged for a single customer complaint. I quit because I was counseled so intently with brow beating, intimidation, and bullying I nearly fell apart. Intimidation and bullying are not restricted to only children, this is also an adult workplace issue.

I don't even know if this is a corporate policy to eliminate older females in the workforce. The corporation could be working politically to get rid of older female employees proving to the nation that the corporation is offering new jobs ending high unemployment. How would one know if it was a corporate policy or not? If it is a corporate policy and a bullying assistant manager is following corporate policy, then he just might see rapid advancement because he is doing an excellent job. The media receives news that a retail corporation just hired 60,000 employees in a year. Did the corporation release that 75,000 employees quit or were fired in a year?

Like the other associate, I quit. I quit under duress. I could not work in such a hostile, sexual gender, age, and race biased environment. The intimidation tactics did work on me. My blood pressure shot up raising my blood sugars to sky high limits. I had a violent headache for days and could not sleep. I could not bring my blood pressure down for days. Did I mention I am a diabetic and have Coronary Artery Disease with a stent in my heart artery? This last round of abusive counseling nearly did me in. Maybe it still will. I can also see where this type of intense abusive intimidation could cause someone to commit suicide. But even if intimidation and bullying are negative tactics, is it a corporate policy? Who will ever know or care? Does an economic slave have any rights or value? Of course not!

The use of intimidation and bullying sets up employee against employee is another negative tactic used in the corporate world. The losers are the employees under duress by no fault of theirs, but pulled into a battle of control by a bully. Is it just one bully, or is it dictates of a corporate bully? I would really like to know. Going against intimidation could indeed put jobs at risk.

Corporations actually empower bully managers to intimidate and create a fear environment because there are no guidelines to regarding management behavior. There is also no recourse for any worker to fight intimidation and bullying from management. Any employee that tries to explain the fear environment and heavy hands of management end up losing their jobs, or forced to quit due to unbearable pressure from management. Legally, bullying is impossible to prove without recorded documentation that simply cannot happen in a "counseling" session. It is always a he said, she said controversy that ends up with the corporation standing behind the abusive manager.

There is always at least one bully in the managerial mix. Are psychological tests done on potential managers? It is my belief that the only requirement of today's managers is that they make numbers follow the path of corporate directives. No people skills are required.

The worst part is bullies do really get off on being a bully and know they can get away with it. One way or another these previous workers I discussed were harassed, bullied, intimidated, fed up and left and or discharged by a managerial bully. I have like my predecessors been harassed, intimidated, and bullied. It has been one thing or another and the bully never ceases to harass at any given chance. I am an older, Caucasian, overweight, female with health issues. Is it just me that sees a pattern here? I can only ask myself if it is just one manager or just one store, how does a manager get away with it? Does a store manager condone this? Is that what the store manager, district manager, regional manager, or corporate office condones and or set as current policy? There is a sense in the world of corporate America today that the elder are being targeted for job elimination. There are laws against such discriminatory practices, but the corporations easily side step them by creating infractions of rules that are exaggerated and expounded on from mere nothingness. Unfortunately I sometimes believe even the government of this country is a bully against its people to keep their power. I don't believe our government cares about such violations of the laws they put in place. I see no difference in the current economic slaves and the blindsided founding fathers of the antebellum slavery years.

A bullying manager instills fear and or anger in almost all of the workers in a store. He can without restrictions continually spy on employees and haul them in for the most minor of infractions, if you can call them infractions. Those that are favored by management generally do as they please, come and go disregarding instructions, respect, dress code, and schedules.

The dress codes of retail corporations are explicit. Yet, managers flagrantly ignore certain infractions and sometimes violate the dress code themselves. In any retail corporate store you might notice some employees dress well and other stores the workers look like slobs, even if it is a similar or same retailer. The foot requirement is footwear that is treaded for safety from slipping and the entire foot is covered, some managers ignore the rule or allow others to violate the rule, but enforce the rule on others. Young men wear the current fashion of underwear exposure. This is a clear violation of dress code, as well as hair dreads in the extremes, but these are not only acceptable in one store, some of the supervisors wear the same style fad. On the other hand, sexual bias dictates that women are more subject to dress code rules than males. Women are more likely to get singled out and reprimanded for dress code violations of any sort than men. In the case of women, it is the female employees that report violations and demand action on them, then men. It appears that men are allowed to do and wear what they will.

In conclusion - slavery lives on without recourse or hope for the slaves. There is nothing we can do to end slavery since we are as entwined in its deadly vines as the slaves of our early history years. We have no unions to fight for us. And no unions are allowed in the corporate retail world. It would be wonderful if retail corporations truly were self regulatory so there would be no need for labor unions.

We are so mind controlled that we have no recourse until we are destroyed or an occupying foreign country takes over our government. Until then the corporation is all powerful. The corporation is the massah, and we must succumb. Sadly, when a new world power eventually consumes corporate America, we will simply have a new massah and still be a slave. The only hope would be a catastrophic natural destruction that would allow a rebirth of the human race. Humans would again have a value for skills and labor as it happened after the Black Plague nearly destroyed two thirds of Europe.

The United States is spiraling quickly downward. Just six months ago it was only one third of our work force was under the poverty level. At the writing of this book, it is one half. Average wages are plummeting every year, while our spendable income decreases at exponential rates. The wealthy 2% now own 80% of American wealth. The massah is profiting well under the slaves' labor.

This book is a wakeup call to the corporations and the oligarchy they have created. With placing only value on perceived wealth and no value to humanity, you are leading your own way to self destruction. When you own everything and nothing is left for others, the others lose all hope. When there is no hope humanity loses all incentives to achieve. The society falls apart and breaks down. When there is no society left you only have chaos. Where there is chaos, the wealth you have has no value.

When you empower bullies you create anger. Anger is negative and destructive for the employee and the corporation. Anger creates crisis. The crisis could lead to suicide, shooting, and or both.

The economic slavery must end, but it can only end by the ending of this current gluttonous oligarchy. Only the powerful oligarchy can stop their destructive path. Corporations must return value to their workers. Corporations must not only demand respect and reverence, but give it to earn it. Corporations must invest in their tools with livable wage. A livable wage gives power to purchase product, the product corporations produce.

Corporations must re-invest in themselves with new equipment, innovation, and green technology. Merely reinvesting profits in digital wealth produces nothing. Without product the inflated balloon bursts and no one has anything. Cruel practices, intimidation, bullying, and harassment only breed fear. With fear corporations breed contempt. When contempt peaks, there is violence. There is more violence in this world and you the corporations are directly responsible for it because of corporate gluttony.

Corporations must live up to loyalty and do not expect it, demand it, or force it. Loyalty is redeemed by those who earn it. Loyalty is found only in leadership, not intimidation, harassment, or bullying.

Wake up Corporations, you are no longer walking down the path of self destruction, you are in an uncontrollable roll towards self destruction. You may not care about any of your slaves, and are just concerned about your digital profits, but your destruction is just as near as your slaves end. Your power and control is only as great as the people who work to help you grow.

This book is a last great hope to reach people to see how gluttony is destroying humanity. Humanity's destruction can only lead to a violent end to the corporate wealth. Can the tide of negativity be turned? Corporation giants can make a difference without losing their wealth. The workers aren't really concerned about great wealth. The workers only want a livable wage, loyalty and acknowledgment of their work with pay increases adjusted to cost of living, a security of income, and security of a comfortable retirement in an elder age.

Personally, I have worked fifty years. I want to retire. I want to give the youth my job. I want to sit back, relax and enjoy the roses. I want to train the youth to ensure a good employee to a company, learning from the youth's suggestions and working together for good changes. I would love to leave a heritage of proof that good work ethics pay off in the end. I would love to prove that loyalty pays off. Economically I cannot retire or offer advice of ethics and loyalty. Instead I offer this book to employees and corporations a chance to view one concept of today's world. Truly Mahatma Gandhi's words are powerful – "We must be the change we desire in the world." This book is my one step in obtaining the change I would like in the world. You may agree or disagree with this book, which is unimportant. What matters is that it made you think. Thank you for sharing my thoughts.

I love to quote this bible passage, "What is a man profit if he gain the whole world, but lose his soul?"

Epilogue

As with all non fiction books, the content is a perception. Everyone perceives a situation in a different light. This book is a result of my perceived observances and does not necessarily reflect the perception of other workers or all corporations. I have worked for several large retail corporations over the past thirty years and they seem to fall in my perceived patterns of economic slavery. I do not want to indicate in any way that all who read these lines should agree with my perceptions. After all, we all see things differently and that makes us unique.

It is my hope that corporations read and understand these observances to take action for a positive change in the American workplace. A positive environment can only benefit the corporations and still allow them to keep their wealth. A happy environment is a productive environment, but it must be a factually good environment.

Have you had an economic slavery issue you want to share? Please write to paytonlee1949@gmail.com.

www.ingramcontent.com/pod-product-compliance
Lightning Source LLC
Chambersburg PA
CBHW071620170526
45166CB00003B/1126